Volume 11

MODERN FIGHTING AIRCRAFT

B-1B

Mike Spick

An Arco Military Book
Prentice Hall Press · New York

A Salamander Book

Published in 1986 by Prentice Hall Press
A Division of Simon & Schuster, Inc.
Gulf + Western Building
One Gulf + Western Plaza
New York, N.Y. 10023

Originally published in the United Kingdom by Salamander Books Ltd

10 9 8 7 6 5 4 3 2 1

First Prentice Hall Press Edition

PRENTICE HALL PRESS is a trademark of Simon & Schuster, Inc.

All correspondence concerning the content of this book should be addressed to Salamander Books Ltd.,
52 Bedford Row, London,
United Kingdom WC1R 4LR.

This book may not be sold outside the United States of America and Canada.

Library of Congress Cataloging-in-Publication Data

Spick, Mike
  B-1B

  (Modern fighting aircraft; v. 11)
  "An Arco aviation book."
  1. B-1 bomber.   I. Title.   II. Title: B-One B.
III. Series.
UG1242.B6S673   1986   358.4'2   86-12333
ISBN 0-13-055237-2

Credits

Project Manager: Ray Bonds

Editor: Bernard Fitzsimons

Designed by Lim & Lim

Diagrams: Pete Coote, Danny Lim, Phil Adams and Mike Badrocke

Contents

Acknowledgements

The author and publisher are grateful to all those who have contributed information and illustrations to this book. Photograph sources are credited on page 64, but particular thanks are due to Earl Blount, Lyn Castorina, Jack L. Hefley, Mike Matthews and Scott L. White of Rockwell International; Major Ron Hinkle and Major George H. Peck, HQ Aeronautical Systems Division, Wright-Patterson AFB; Dr Richard Hallion, Edwards AFB; DoD Public Affairs, the Pentagon; Major William H. Austin, USAF Office of Public Affairs; Dwight E. Weber of the General Electric Company; Peter B. Dakan of Boeing Military Airplane Company; Richard L. Palmay of Eaton Corporation AIL Division; Robert F. Dorr; and Air Force Magazine.

Author

Mike Spick was born in London less than three weeks before the Spitfire made its maiden flight. Educated at Churchers College, Petersfield, he later entered the construction industry and carried out considerable work on RAF airfields. An interest in wargaming led him to a close study of air warfare and a highly successful first book, *Air Battles in Miniature* (Patrick Stephens, 1978). His subsequent work includes a historical study of the evolution of air combat tactics, *Fighter Pilot Tactics* (Patrick Stephens, 1983), co-authorship of the Salamander Book *Modern Air Combat* (with Bill Gunston, 1983), and three earlier volumes in this series: *F-4 Phantom II* (with Doug Richardson, 1984), *F/A-18 Hornet* (1984) and *F-14 Tomcat* (1985).

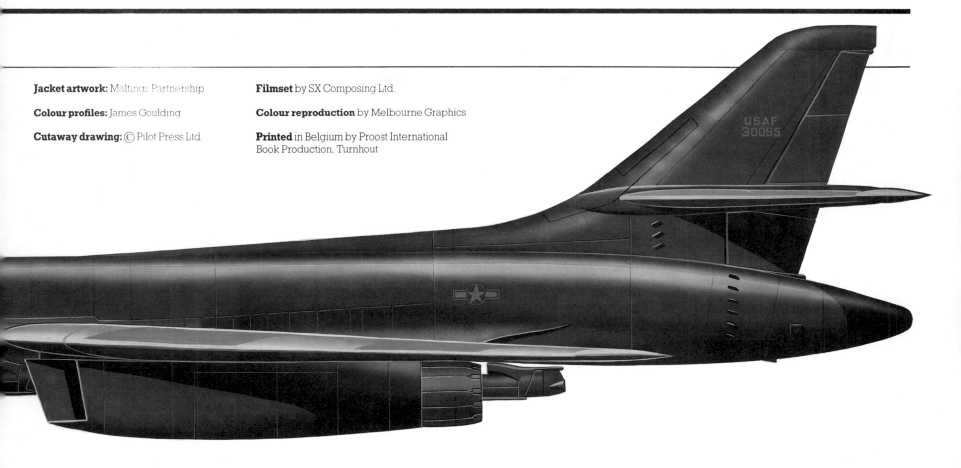

Jacket artwork: Maltings Partnership

Colour profiles: James Goulding

Cutaway drawing: © Pilot Press Ltd.

Filmset by SX Composing Ltd.

Colour reproduction by Melbourne Graphics

Printed in Belgium by Proost International Book Production, Turnhout

Introduction

The gestation period of the B-1 has been long and difficult even by modern standards. The aircraft was conceived in 1965 after five years of study programmes, the contract was placed on June 5, 1970, and the first aircraft flew on December 23, 1974. The production programme was subsequently cancelled by the Carter Administration, only to be reinstated, albeit in a different though externally similar form during President Reagan's first term in office, and initial operating capability was finally achieved in 1986.

During its chequered career it has been called many things, not all of them flattering: the last of the dinosaurs, an essential leg of the nuclear deterrent triad, a threat to world peace, too expensive, tremendously capable, too vulnerable and – perhaps most insulting of all – an interim solution. Perhaps the most misleading label to have been applied is that of bomber, a word that evokes a big, vulnerable aircraft plodding through the skies at the mercy of both fighters and surface-to-air missiles as it seeks to drop old-fashioned gravity bombs onto a fixed target.

Both the tax-paying public and the politicians knew what a bomber was, though the military did not seem so sure, and for many years controversy abounded as to the exact role of the B-1 and the qualities it should possess. This uncertainty was reflected in the record number of acronyms that the project collected during the early years, a phenomenon that served only to muddy the waters still further.

Two main issues arise. First, can a carrier of strategic weapons penetrate a modern air defence system without incurring an unacceptable level of attrition? Second, has it any significant advantage over the ICBM, the SLBM and the cruise missile? The answer to the first question is that no-one really knows: we can only guess. The answer to the second is an unqualified affirmative, at least in the political sense, since it allows a much greater degree of flexibility.

The final answer will only be known in 40 or 50 years: if the world is still unravaged by nuclear war, the B-1B will have played the part for which it was intended – not by going to war, but by its presence.

The Manned Bomber

It is easy to regard the manned strategic bomber as an anachronism. Intercontinental ballistic missiles allow a fast strike to be made against almost any part of the globe: by comparison, the response of the strategic bomber is almost tortoise-like. Moreover, no effective defence is yet possible against the big missiles with their multiple warheads, whereas the bomber is faced with a combination of fighter and missile defences that, over the last quarter of a century, have made it seem increasingly vulnerable. The question is therefore one of credibility: how viable a proposition is the B-1B?

World War II in Europe ended with Germany in ruins and, on the far side of the world, Japan well on the way to the same fate. Then, in August 1945, a single nuclear weapon dropped from a single bomber over Hiroshima was followed by a second bomb over Nagasaki. These devastating attacks effectively finished the war, and with them the strategic bomber came of age. The destructive power of the new weapons had made it totally convincing. There could be no further argument.

The early carriers of nuclear weapons were the USAF Boeing B-29, which also saw service with the RAF as the Washington, and its Soviet copy, the Tupolev Tu-4. Normal attack altitudes and speeds were something in excess of 30,000ft (9,000m) and 200kts (370km/h) – far short of their maximum stated performance figures, but necessary to achieve a worthwhile operational radius. At these heights and speeds they were fairly safe from interception by piston-engined fighters, which took up to 30 minutes to reach attack altitudes, but vulnerable to the new generation of jet fighters. In the strategic role their range was such as to rule out the possibility of fighter escort, and while they could fly in close forma-

tion for mutual protection during much of the mission, when the time came to attack they were forced to split up and go their separate ways.

The next operational use of B-29s was for conventional bombing during the Korean War. They proved vulnerable to jet fighters in daylight, even with fighter escorts, and were forced to seek the cover of darkness. In turn, this caused a resumption of the electronic war waged over Germany a decade earlier but which had lapsed after 1945.

The factor which had traditionally made the bomber vulnerable to the fighter was the disparity in performance that allowed the fighter to reach the bomber's altitude and overtake it. The arithmetic was simple: detection of a bomber at a mere 50nm (93km) range gave defending fighters some 15 minutes to scramble, reach the bomber's altitude and intercept it before it could reach their airfield. And as detection distance increased so did the time available for interception. It should be noted that intercepting a B-29 was no pushover, and actually shooting it down was something else again. But as the probability of the bomber completing its mission was eroded, so too was its credibility.

The technical advances that gave the jet fighter ascendancy over the B-29 were also applied to bomber design; within a few years USAF heavy bomber squadrons were equipped with, in turn, the gigantic ten-engined mixed power B-36D, the six-jet swept-wing B-47, and finally the eight-engined B-52 Stratofortress, for more than 30 years a principal component Strategic Air Command's contribution to America's nuclear deterrent force.

New performance levels

For interceptors, the B-52 was a totally different proposition from the B-29. The new bomber's operational altitude was one-third higher and its cruising speed about double that of the latter. As a consequence, while reaction times for the defending fighters were halved, they had to climb far higher to intercept. Furthermore, if ground control failed to position the fighters correctly it would take them far longer to catch up, even assuming they had sufficient fuel, and in many cases they would not.

Military aircraft design is a dynamic process, and by the time a prototype leaves the ground for the first time new shapes appearing on drawing boards

Above: The world's first strategic air-to-surface missile was the Bell GAM-63A Rascal, which saw service between 1957 and 1959. Supersonic, with a range of 75 miles (121km), it is seen here being test launched from a DB-47E Stratojet.

are intended to render it obsolete. The B-52 was not expected to be any exception to a clear trend: bombers needed to survive to carry out their mission, survival was enhanced by evading interception by fighters, and interception was evaded by flying higher and faster. There was nothing new about this. The higher and faster progression had been established during World War I, and the technology of the 1950s simply allowed it to proceed faster than ever before.

The USAF's next strategic bomber, the Convair B-58 Hustler, was designed to fly its mission at over 50,000ft (15,200m) and to maintain supersonic speeds for more than 1,000nm (1,850km): the initial penetration would be made at high subsonic speed, culminating in a Mach 2 dash over the target, and a supersonic dash could also be used to penetrate heavily defended areas. The Hustler entered service with Strategic Air Command in 1960, and for reasons which will be touched upon later was phased out 10 years later.

The last American strategic bomber in the ever higher, ever faster tradition was North American Rockwell's XB-70 Valkyrie, intended to fly its entire mission at 80,000ft (24,400m) and Mach 3. At that speed and altitude it was detectable and its course was fairly predictable, but travelling at just under 29nm (53km) per minute and an altitude of 13nm (24km) it would have posed a formidable task for the manned interceptor. However, just as engines, airframes, avionics and weaponry had made giant strides, so had costs, and Valkyrie was cancelled in 1960 despite very encouraging trials.

The fly in the ointment was the missile, or more properly the rocket. Both projectiles and guidance systems had made tremendous progress, and many people

Left: The gigantic Convair B-36D was the link between earlier piston-engined bombers and later fast jet types, being powered by six piston engines with four jets for takeoff and over-the-target dash speed.

Right: The long-range stand-off missile reduced the time that the bomber was at risk to the defences. A B-52G launches a GAM-77 Hound Dog, which could carry a 1MT warhead for up to 710 miles (1,143km).

forecast that the missile would replace both the manned bomber and the manned interceptor. To be fair, the prospects of this happening looked bright. Giant ballistic rockets could carry nuclear and thermonuclear warheads over vast distances with a fair degree of accuracy in a matter of minutes, and were unstoppable by any known means. Clever guidance systems enabled other rockets to follow unerringly and destroy manned aeroplanes. At least, that was the theory. In practice it didn't quite work out, but at the time it looked perfectly possible.

One immediate result was that the new wonder weapons inherited the funding that might otherwise have been used to build more and better aeroplanes. It cast doubt on the viability of manned fighters and bombers, and made some people wonder whether air warfare as it had developed during the previous half-century was an evolutionary aberration. In future, missiles were to deliver the strategic attacks, while the old fashioned flying machine would be ruthlessly hacked from the sky with robot-like precision by defensive missiles. The aeroplane still had a tactical role to play over the battlefield, but as a

strategic weapon it was finished. Or so it was thought in some circles.

Certainly the high flying strategic bomber was beginning to look distinctly vulnerable, a view that was reinforced when Gary Powers' U-2 was shot down by an SA-2 missile over the Soviet Union in May 1960. While the destruction of a single U-2 did not automatically mean that a massed bomber force flying at a lower altitude and using the latest electronic countermeasures would be decimated, it was a clear pointer to the future. The time was sure to come when the defences would have a distinct advantage over the high-altitude bomber.

Contemporary estimates of the effectiveness of the SA-2 'Guideline' varied between 80 and 95 per cent. Later experience was to show that the estimates were an order of magnitude too high; they derived partially from theory and partially from test results, both of which

Above: The B-58 Hustler was designed to penetrate at high altitudes and high subsonic speeds, culminating in an extended Mach 2 dash over the target. It entered service in 1960 but was unsuitable for low-level missions and was phased out in 1970.

Above: The ultimate high-speed, high-altitude bomber was the North American XB-70 Valkyrie, designed to fly the entire mission at Mach 3 and at 80,000ft (24,383m), where it would have been beyond the reach of defending interceptors.

Below: The Valkyrie is seen here in Mach 3 cruise configuration, with the wingtips folded down to give high-speed stability. This state-of-the-art bomber was cancelled, mainly because of the predicted lethality of new missile air defence systems.

tend to be misleading: theory tends not to work in practice, while test firings are conducted in a sterile environment by people with a vested interest in making them work. But at the time the future of the manned bomber looked bleak.

In the event, the Nuclear Triad concept of ICBMs, SLBMs and manned bombers was adopted. ICBMs were tied to fixed bases whose locations were known, and they were vulnerable to a preemptive strike by enemy ICBMs. SLBMs launched from under the sea were safer, although shorter in range, but they had the inherent disadvantage that only a small fraction of the force could be on station at any given moment, and it was impossible to be absolutely certain that they had not been detected. The bomber is also vulnerable – Pearl Harbor is never very far below the surface of the American military mind – but keeping a handful of bombers in the air, armed and ready to go, meant the bomber force could never be totally wiped out by a surprise attack.

The Triad concept had some basic advantages. Any surprise attack would need to hit all three elements simul-taneously and targeting all three elements in all locations would be very complicated and tremendously difficult, while defence against the Triad involves protection against three different forms of attack, so that the defence against any single one is diluted.

Manned bomber advantages

There were further arguments in favour of the manned bomber. Firstly, there could be no guarantee that a conventional war might not have to be fought at some stage, perhaps against a less technically advanced nation, in which the strategic bomber could be used to advantage in a conventional (non-nuclear) role. Secondly, in times of tension, strategic bomber forces could rapidly be deployed to sensitive areas, thus expressing the determination of the nation to resist, and as a last resort a full scale strike could be launched yet still recalled at the last minute. An ICBM, by contrast, was irrecoverable and unstoppable, leaving the politicians no time for second thoughts. More immediately, there were a lot of bombers in existence or under construction. To scrap them, along with their supporting infrastructure, could have been disastrous not only in terms of national morale and the economy, but because a potential aggressor might interpret such a move as indicative of a lessening of the collective will to resist.

The performance of the B-58 was sufficient to make it a formidable opponent for some years to come, but only 116 were built, including training variants. Valkyrie could hardly have entered service before 1970 and – electronic countermeasures notwithstanding – could not be expected to constitute a credible threat for long in the face of improving defensive systems. Its colossal expense meant that procurement would be low, and the whole concept of a trisonic bomber was dubious.

Following the Valkyrie's cancellation, efforts were concentrated on giving added survivability, and therefore credibility, to SAC's principal bomber, the B-52. Nearly 750 had been built, of which the first had been delivered in June 1955; it was a relatively new type, and had a lot of operational life left in it if only it could be made capable of pen-etrating the defences. ECM kit went without saying; other means of enhancing survivability included stand-off missiles, which would allow it to attack the target from a distance rather than overfly it, and defence suppression missiles to blast a hole in enemy defensive systems through which it could penetrate.

Another interesting idea was the Quail decoy missile, whose radar signature was enhanced to simulate that of the parent bomber and which followed a pre-programmed course to distract the defenders from the real bomber. Of course, gadgets like Quail are nice to have, and each one launched could have diverted an attack, but only a limited number of decoys could be carried and each one reduced the effective warload.

The nub of the matter lay in detection, and in defence reaction times. Bombers generally have large radar reflective surfaces, so they can be detected from great distances, and the quest for ever greater heights and speeds had some drawbacks. High altitude was effective against interceptors, whose time to height had become critical, but less so against SAMs, which took off vertically after little preparation.

At the same time, height made bombers visible from further away. For all practical purposes, radar emissions travel in straight lines, so the horizon blocks the line of travel; a bomber flying at a constant altitude follows the curvature of the earth, and the higher it flies the sooner it will appear over the radar horizon, increasing the warning time given to the defences. ECM could help the bomber to remain undetected, but it was far from being the whole answer. Very high speeds reduced the defenders' reaction time, but curtailed the bomber's powers of manoeuvre and made its course more predictable. Something new was needed.

Low-level penetration

The response, designed to reduce detection ranges and defence reaction times, as well as the effectiveness of surface-to-air missiles and fighters, was really very simple: penetration would be undertaken at low level, below the radar horizon.

Effective defence against the bomber was entirely dependent on effective detection: any reduction increased the bomber's chance of completing the mission in proportion. The SAMs of that era were not designed to engage low-flying targets, and at low levels the interceptor fighters lost much of their ostensibly overwhelming performance advantage. Naturally there was a price to be paid – fuel burn is much greater at low altitudes, reducing radius of action, though long-range attack weapons helped make good the deficiency – but there was a degree of compensation in the fact that the defending fighters would be in

Above left: To confuse the defences, B-52s could each carry two GAM-72 Quail decoys, fitted with reflectors in their noses to augment their radar signatures to that of a B-52 and equipped with jamming devices. Flying a pre-programmed course, Quail's function was to distract the defences from the real bomber; it was phased out in the late 1970s.

Left: The first aircraft in SAC service to be fully capable of low-level all-weather penetration, achieved using terrain-following radar, was the FB-111, seen here carrying four SRAMs. The FB-111 also proved the operational validity of variable geometry, and much of the technology of the B-1 was based on experience gained with this aircraft.

even worse straights. With full afterburner they would consume fuel at a colossal rate while barely reaching Mach 1. By contrast, the speed of the bomber at low level would be little affected.

The shooting down of Powers' U-2 had little or no effect on the decision to switch to low level penetration; SAC had initiated it some months earlier, and the process was complete after about three years. Both the British and the French nuclear deterrent forces also switched to low-level penetration at the same time.

The RAF's adoption of night bombing early in World War II had represented an attempt to make the raiders invisible to the defenders, and the switch to low-level penetration in the early 1960s was aimed at the same target, although low level in a B-52 was not at all the same thing as low level in a modern aircraft such as Tornado GR.1.

Another approach to invisibility was represented by the use of ECM to blind defenders, an interesting illustration of which came in the later stages of the Vietnam War. Before April 1972 strategic targets in the North were attacked by tactical fighter-bombers, while B-52s were engaged in bombing targets further south. The obvious inference was that the B-52s were considered too vulnerable to attack the heavily defended targets in North Vietnam. However, during the Linebacker II campaign at the end of 1972, B-52 raids on the North were mounted under cover of darkness, assisted by jamming and defence sup-

pression aircraft. The B-52s flew at the optimum engagement height of the SA-2 missiles, which were launched at them in large numbers, but instead of the slaughter predicted some years earlier, only about two per cent of the B-52 sorties were lost, while the SA-2s' kill ratio was also only about two per cent. MiG-21 fighters also attempted to intervene, losing two of their number for no result.

It should be remembered that these were conventional (iron) bomb attacks, and that the bombers flew in cells of three to maximize their ECM effect, whereas had they been carrying out a nuclear strike they would have flown

singly and at low altitude. What difference that would have made is difficult to predict, although it seems likely that casualties would not have been too severe.

To summarize, the quest for ever-increasing altitude and speed had been abandoned in favour of trying to sneak past the defences at low level using intensive ECM and on-board defence suppression weapons. The aircraft used were already in the inventory rather than being of a purpose-built type. Valkyrie, at that time the most advanced bomber in the world, had been abandoned, and a new bomber was needed: the road to the B-1B had started.

Above: The B-52 in its different forms has been the mainstay of SAC since 1955. Its internal bomb bays can hold a formidable load, while even more weapons can be carried externally, as this B-52G, preparing to take off with a dozen SRAMs on underwing pylons, demonstrates.

Below: As the B-1B enters service, the elderly B-52 will be relegated to the role of stand-off cruise missile carrier. Its main weapon will be the AGM-86 ALCM, seen here being test launched, whose range is sufficient to allow the bomber to keep well clear of the defences.

Development

The plethora of names and acronyms applied to the B-1 during its protracted gestation could give the impression that the US defence procurement staff did not really know what they were about. An insight into the problems was given by Lt Gen Kelly H. Burke in an address to the NAC in March 1982: "I've always thought that if military history teaches us anything, it ought to teach us humility, because we never have been very good at predicting the next war . . . we've not always done a good job in acquiring the right sort of weapons to fight those wars." The years of chopping and changing that preceded the B-1B's service entry represented a determined effort to get it right.

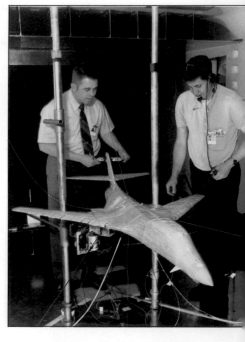

AMSA 1967

By 1967 the Advanced Manned Strategic Aircraft layout depicted here had emerged from a plethora of radical designs. The fuselage is a broad lifting body, while the fully swept angle of the wing is a truly remarkable 75°.

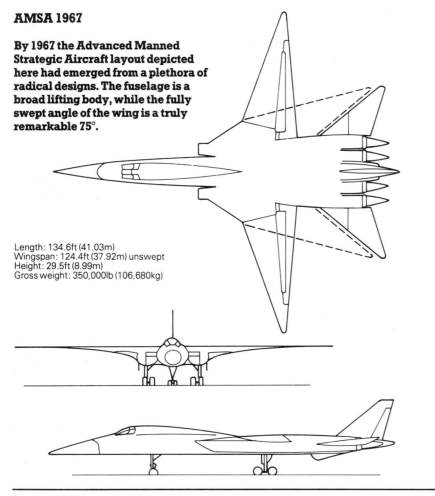

Length: 134.6ft (41.03m)
Wingspan: 124.4ft (37.92m) unswept
Height: 29.5ft (8.99m)
Gross weight: 350,000lb (106,680kg)

The shooting down of Gary Powers' U-2 over the Soviet Union in May 1960 did not immediately invalidate the high-altitude bomber, but it was an indication that the route to survival lay in avoiding radar detection by flying below the radar horizon, and in 1961 the United States Air Force initiated exploratory studies of a new concept, the Subsonic Low Altitude Bomber, or SLAB. The SLAB studies were followed in 1962 by Project Forecast, a USAF examination of the force structure requirements for the strategic triad for the period through to the 1980s: concluded in 1969, it made a strong case for the retention of the manned bomber as an essential part of both deterrent and conventional forces.

In 1963, while the USAF pursued new research on the Extended Range Strategic Aircraft (ERSA) and Low Altitude Manned Penetrator (LAMP), other studies were carried out by industry on government contract under the titles Advanced Manned Penetrator (AMP) and Advanced Manned Penetrating Strategic System (AMPSS). AMP consisted of preliminary design and evaluation of the technical and economic feasibility of four basic mission concepts: low altitude subsonic; subsonic low altitude and medium supersonic high altitude; subsonic low altitude and high supersonic high altitude; and V/STOL. The two main questions to be answered were essentially what the Air Force could reasonably expect in a given time

Above: Wind tunnel tests vary from the simple examination of airflow patterns to the very exotic. The amount of wiring attached to this B-1 model indicates the latter.

scale, and what it could afford. At an early stage the second solution seems to have been favoured, as the AMPSS study concerned the optimization of this concept.

During 1965 the AMP and AMPSS studies were concluded and a new one started on the Advanced Manned Strategic Aircraft, or AMSA, later lampooned as "America's Most Studied Aircraft". The AMSA programme lasted for the next four years, and in essence consisted of the development of a point design in a flexible manner. The AMSA study was carried out by three airframe companies, Boeing, General Dynamics, and North American Rockwell, and funded by the Air Force.

The primary mission of AMSA was officially stated as being to deter nuclear war through the ability to survive an enemy first strike, successfully penetrate enemy defences (both actual and projected) and accurately deliver either stand-off or laydown weapons on both military and industrial targets, and the basic point design required that initial survivability, penetration capability and payload/range be better than those of the B-52, at that time the mainstay of Strategic Air Command.

AMSA 1968

By 1968 the engines had been relocated from the rear to a mid position, a more orthodox fuselage had emerged and the wings had been totally redesigned. Sealing the trailing edge glove looks difficult.

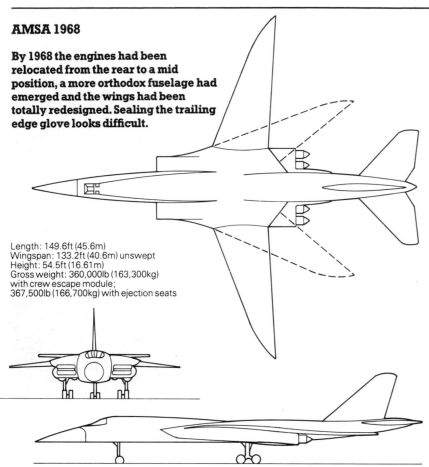

Length: 149.6ft (45.6m)
Wingspan: 133.2ft (40.6m) unswept
Height: 54.5ft (16.61m)
Gross weight: 360,000lb (163,300kg)
with crew escape module;
367,500lb (166,700kg) with ejection seats

B-1 proposal 1969

The 1969 B-1 proposal bears little resemblance to its ancestor of just one year earlier: the wing is now set low, with podded paired engines, and the intakes are side by side rather than stacked vertically.

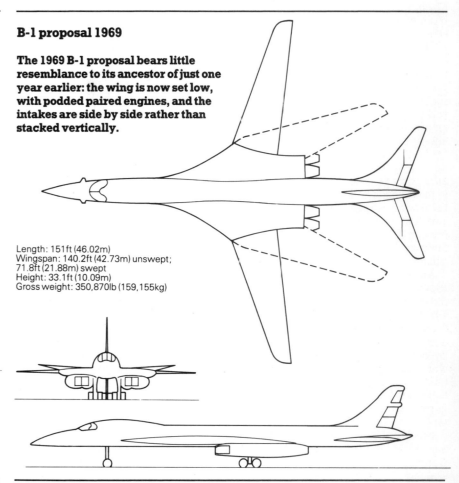

Length: 151ft (46.02m)
Wingspan: 140.2ft (42.73m) unswept;
71.8ft (21.88m) swept
Height: 33.1ft (10.09m)
Gross weight: 350,870lb (159,155kg)

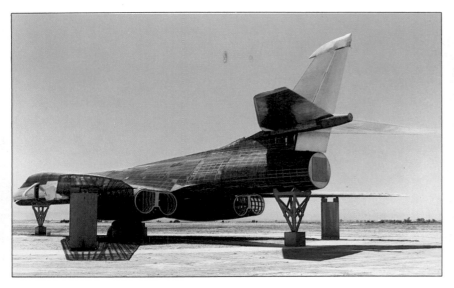

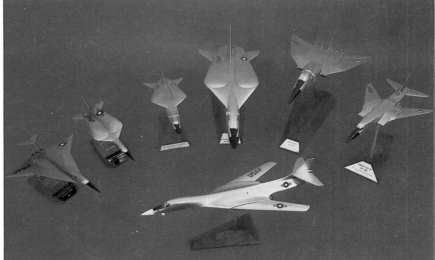

Above: The B-1 mockup is seen here at an early stage. Access to the interior is through a door on the side of the nose, but this was not a feature of the finished product.

Above right: Two fixed wing models are shown, along with three AMSA proposals whose wing sweep angles exceed 90° to form rhomboidal lifting bodies. AMSA 1968 is at far right.

The earlier studies had shown that the best chance of successful penetration of a heavily defended area lay in high subsonic speed at low altitude while supersonic performance at high altitude gave greater flexibility, as well as reducing the transit time through lightly defended areas. This was the point design around which AMSA was developed, and in November 1969 the USAF was able to issue Requests for Proposals. The three companies that had participated in the AMSA studies made their submissions, and in June of the following year Rockwell International, as North American Rockwell had become, were selected as B-1 system contractors.

Winning design

An interesting development process had led to the winning design. The most modern weapons available at the time were the Short Range Attack Missile (SRAM), for which Boeing Aerospace were awarded a contract in October 1966, and another Boeing product, the Subsonic Cruise Armed Decoy (SCAD), which was designed to be interchangeable with SRAM. The B-52 was intended to carry eight of these missiles internally on a rotary launcher, and consideration

of cost-effectiveness dictated that the B-1 be able to do better, the obvious way ahead being multiple launchers. Accordingly it was decided to mount three rotary launchers internally, giving three times the striking power of the B-52, but since the relationship between weight and cost dictated that AMSA was to be a rather smaller aircraft than the B-52 tripling the internal weapons load was going to be difficult. Some idea of the problem is presented in the following table.

Weight as percentage of the gross	**B-52**	**AMSA**
Structure	22	22
Systems	20	22
Weapons load	5	15
Fuel	53	41
	100	100

The structural percentage had to be held down to the same level as the B-52, even though the aeroplane was smaller. Again, the systems could not be allowed to increase by more than two per cent of the gross weight: even though such extras as terrain-following radar, addi-

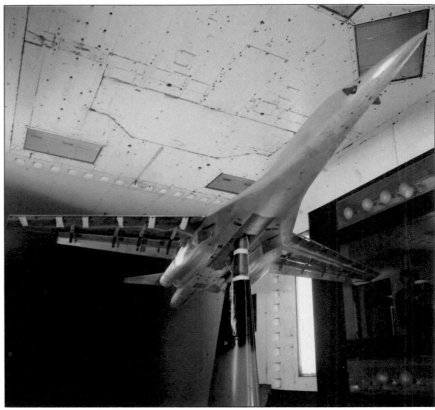

Above: Wind tunnel model of the B-1 showing the leading edge slats and the complicated double translating flaps originally proposed. Also shown are the original horizontally raked supersonic inlets.

Below: The mockup, complete with Strategic Air Command insignia on the nose, against a scenic backdrop with star filter effects. The date is December 1971, some three years before the B-1's maiden flight.

tional penetration aids and extra sensors had to be fitted, the reduction in gross weight meant they actually had to weigh less than those of the B-52. This only left one area in which savings could be made – fuel – so a range comparable to that of the B-52 had to be achieved with a reduction in fuel fraction amounting to 29 per cent.

Matters were further complicated by the decision to use a variable-geometry (VG) wing. This had many operational advantages, allowing short takeoffs and landings, which aided dispersal, while full sweep gave a good configuration for supersonic flight and low gust response, an invaluable quality in the low-level penetration role. On the other hand, it meant that valuable space would be taken up by the wings and their pivots, actuators and hydraulic systems. In terms of weight fraction, VG added to the section called systems. If payload and range were not to suffer, some very interesting tradeoffs would have to be made.

In fact, the first tradeoff had already been made, when vertical takeoff and landing was considered and rejected. If not totally beyond the state of the art at that time, it was certainly considered to carry too high a development risk, while the added weight and cost could only have been balanced by a reduction in

Above: The underside of the rear fuselage of the B-1 contains some interesting compound curves. Here the left fuselage and the inside of the inner left engine nacelle are tufted to examine the airflow.

payload, range or both. In-flight refuelling was always available, but the demands would have been excessive and the increase in the size of the tanker fleet very costly, and while survivability in the event of a surprise attack would have been greatly enhanced, a VTOL bomber ideally needs a VTOL tanker.

Efforts to hold down the structural weight percentage involved the examination of new materials and design concepts. Boron and carbon composites were investigated, along with high-strength steel and aluminium alloys, but the main effort was directed towards the use of titanium. From the design angle, concepts such as blended wing bodies, which permitted maximum structural depth and minimized wetted area, were carefully considered.

Power for AMSA was the subject of a separate programme aimed at a minimum length lightweight afterburning turbofan incorporating a short annular combustor, a short mixer and augmentor, a high temperature turbine and cooled blades. Contracts were let for the

Top: The first B-1A, the flying qualities test vehicle, shown with the SAC nose stripe at medium altitude over the Mojave desert. The barber pole pitot was carried for flight instrumentation reasons only.

development of two technology demonstrator engines, the final choice falling on a General Electric design.

The avionic systems, both offensive and defensive, were to be the most comprehensive yet seen, and keeping the weight percentage down posed a challenge. The main emphasis was on the use of digital systems and multi-function phased array antennas. A development programme on the radar system was established, and a breadboard apparatus was constructed and test flown in a C-135. The avionic systems were obviously going to be very complex and demand a lot of power; a 230-volt electrical system was proposed, combined with a lot of electrical multiplexing, but new technology offered better reliability and general simplification.

Survivability requirements

The need to survive a surprise attack had a considerable impact on systems requirements. The key to survival lay in wide dispersion, and while this would

Above: Final approach to one of the 79 landings made by the first prototype during a career that included 405.3 hours of test flying during the four years that followed its first flight on December 23, 1974.

normally be to SAC bases in the United States, the use of quite small and spartan civil airfields was not discounted in times of political tension. The variable-geometry wing was an advantage in getting in and out of small fields, but there were many other considerations. AMSA had to be stand-alone capable, able to operate with little or no flight line equipment. In the event of an alert, it had to be capable of self-starting, and airborne within a very few minutes. Good communications at the airfield were not essential, as the on-board systems could be used, but what was essential was the ability to check that the bomber was ready to go with all systems available. This was accomplished by means of an on-board Central Integrated Test System (CITS), which provided data on serviceability status.

The final requirement, which bit into the strutural and systems weight percentages, was the need to incorporate nuclear hardening against both blast (for the airframe) and electro-magnetic pulse (EMP) for the avionic systems.

B-1A first prototype (74-0158)

All B-1As were finished originally with white anti-flash paint, but this made them far too visible at low level.

Above: The first B-1A with wings fully swept in a climbing turn at high altitude. What appears to be slight skin wrinkling can be seen aft of the crew area, and there is no transparency in the rear cockpit.

With all these factors taken into consideration, the required mission range had still to be achieved while using a smaller fuel fraction. The high-technology turbofans promised between 10 and 15 per cent better specific fuel consumption than the Pratt & Whitney J57s of the B-52, which contributed greatly to the solution of the problem; the rest had to be down to the aerodynamicists. Once again the variable-sweep wing was the largest single contributing factor, and this was developed from the same NASA data base as that of the F-111.

By 1967 the thousands of configurations had been whittled down and a point design had emerged, though this paper aeroplane bore little resemblance to the B-1 ultimately built. AMSA 1967 was 134.6ft (41.02m) long, 29.5ft (8.99m) high at the single fin, and spanned 124.4ft (37.92m) with the wings at minimum sweep. The four turbofans, located at the rear of the fuselage, were fed from sharply raked two-dimensional intakes set out from the forward fuselage. The single fin was mounted on the end of the

fuselage which projected slightly back behind the engines, and the abiding impression was that it was rather undersized, though it was supplemented by two small ventral fins set on the outside of the twin engine nacelles. The cockpit formed a bulge on the top of the forward fuselage, and was faired gently back almost to the halfway point.

Most remarkable of all in appearance were the wings. The wing gloves commenced just behind the intakes, and were set high, sweeping back at approximately 55°, and the wings themselves were almost perfectly triangular in shape, with lightly rounded tips. At minimum sweep of around 20° the trailing edge actually swept forward, while maximum sweep angle was a spectacular 75°, the wings folding back to form an almost continuous surface with the horizontal stabilizers, which were set in a marginally lower plane than the wings. The wings had a very slight dihedral; the stabilizer a slightly larger one. Despite all efforts, the structural weight percentage had crept up to 24, though the systems were down at 18, as was the weapons load, now 14 per cent, leaving the fuel fraction to make up the difference at 44 per cent. The design gross weight was 350,000lb (158,760kg).

Both the design and the requirements continued to develop. The weapons load

Above: 'Burners cooking, the first B-1A departs Edwards. The rather clumsy wing glove fairing can be seen to advantage from this angle. It was revised on the B-1B.

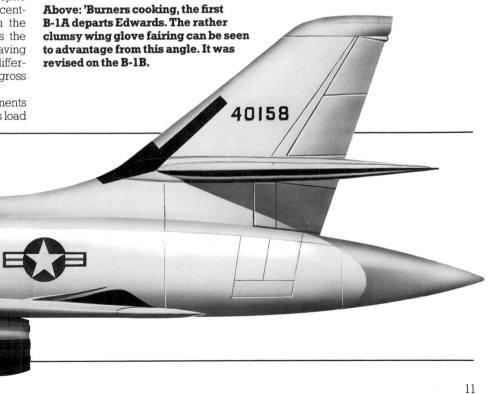

was increased from 24 to 32 SRAMs carried internally, and the point design had to change considerably to accommodate an effective 33 per cent increase. Obviously, on a combat mission, the weapons load is expended, either gradually or fairly rapidly, and this greatly effects the aerodynamic balance of the carrier aircraft. It was therefore necessary to place the engines near the aerodynamic centre of the aircraft rather than at the tail, but this in turn caused other problems, such as heating of the rear fuselage from the engine exhausts, while the location of the horizontal stabilizers had also to be amended.

As a result of these changes, AMSA 1968 bore little likeness to its predecessor of the year before, but had begun to bear a passing resemblance to the future B-1. The length had increased to 149.6ft (45.60m), height to the top of the fin had jumped 46 per cent to 54.5ft (16.61m) while the span at minimum sweep had increased slightly to 133.2ft (40.60m).

The engines were located in pairs in twin nacelles on each side of the fuselage; the intakes showed little change, but were now clearly paired, one on top of the other. The single fin was greatly increased both in height and in area, and moved forward a few feet, while the ventral fins had gone, since there was nowhere to locate them. The cockpit bulge was much more smoothly faired into the fuselage, and the wing gloves, starting high on the intakes and much reduced in size, no longer blended into the fuselage but ended in a fillet above the twin engine nacelles, with the wing sweeping back into the fillet. The wings also had a new shape, a straight leading edge curving gently toward the tip to give a sharp point where it met the trailing edge, which now had a slight sweepback when fully extended.

At this stage the design was beginning to harden, and a great many tradeoff studies were initiated. Cost effectiveness had always been important, and now it became paramount, the basic parameter being relative effectiveness in destroying a specific target complex or system set against the overall system cost. Previous cost comparisons had been based on weight, but the point design, in the form of AMSA 1968, was

now used as the basis of a more comprehensive cost analysis against which tradeoff costs could be compared. Many studies were undertaken, the most important of which were:

(a) Landing gear flotation requirements against dispersal capability (involving a worst-case assessment of small dispersal airfields).

(b) Crew escape module compared with ejection seats. The normal operational crew consisted of four men, but on training missions two instructors would bring the number up to six. Rather surprisingly, the study showed savings using a six-man module based on that of the two-man F-111, which was some 6,750lb (3,062kg) lighter overall, taking into account the individual life support systems. The USAF also felt that crew effectiveness would be greater in the shirt-sleeve environment than in all the normal paraphernalia of flying gear, as efficiency is improved when the crew can communicate with each other direct rather than using communications equipment. A further consideration was that in the event of an ejection at high altitude and high supersonic speeds, the crew module was much more survivable.

(c) CITS capability as compared with AGE (automated ground environment). This was an easy one to resolve, as although the CITS added weight, cost, and complexity to the aircraft, its omission greatly increased the bomber's vulnerability to surprise attack while reducing its credibility as a combat system.

(d) Ride quality against crew effectiveness. As a rule of thumb, the lower the altitude, the rougher the ride. The planned ultra low level penetration at high subsonic speeds gave the best chance of mission success, but subjected the crew to a bone-jarring series of jolts at intervals of two or three seconds. This is uncomfortable in the short term, and for the extended periods that would be necessary for deep penetration, would be so fatiguing as to considerably affect crew efficiency. The answer partly lies in the gust response of the aircraft, the conditioning factors of which are a low aspect ratio and a high wing loading. The AMSA project, with wings fully swept, fulfilled both these conditions admirably

Above: The first B-1A lets it all hang out on finals, giving a good view of the stalky narrow track gear and the movable ramps of the horizontally raked supersonic engine inlet configuration.

Right: The B-1A was intended to have a Mach 2 capability at high altitude. Wings fully swept, the second prototype sets off on a high-speed run, the flared position of the nozzles indicating full throttle.

in terms of design, but the size of the aircraft caused problems, its sheer length tending to induce a whipping motion, with the aircraft flexing as it rode the gusts. There were two possible ways to reduce this motion to acceptable levels: either to make the fuselage much more rigid, though the weight penalty of doing this was prohibitive; or to use low altitude ride control, in which small sensor actuated vanes were mounted on the sides of the nose, reacting automatically to gusts and smoothing out the ride.

(e) Nuclear hardness versus initial survival. This is a sensitive area, and no firm information was released on this study, but it seems reasonable to speculate that nuclear hardening beyond a certain point demands extra weight and a longer takeoff run, reducing dispersal capability, which in turn reduces the probability of surviving a surprise attack.

By 1969 the years of study were ready to bear fruit. Concept definition was complete, and the Department of Defense authorized the USAF to proceed

Left: Three B-1A's on the flight line was a rare sight. The second B-1A, restored to flying order after eight months of load testing during 1975, is in the foreground, with the first and third aircraft to left and right respectively.

further. Until this point, most of the studies had been concerned with relative cost effectiveness, and two things were certain: this would be the most studied and easily the most expensive combat aircraft in the world. As related earlier, Requests for Proposals were issued, the submissions were studied, and the weapon system contract was awarded to Rockwell. No longer just a project, the design had ceased to be AMSA, and had become the B-1.

The Rockwell proposal bore a close resemblance to the B-1 as it finally flew. Compared to AMSA 1968, overall length was slightly up at 151ft (46.02m), height to the top of the fin was considerably reduced, to 33.1ft (10.09m), while span at minimum sweep had grown to 140.2ft (42.73m).

In plan view the Low Altitude Ride Control (LARC) vanes were clearly visible on either side of the nose just ahead of the cockpit, area ruling was readily apparent for the first time, and the leading edges of the wing glove boxes, freed now from proximity to the engine intakes, described a gentle concave curve outward from the fuselage. The wings, more blunted at the tips, ranged from a minimum sweep angle of

15° to a maximum of 75°, producing a rather odd shoulder effect reminiscent of an F-14 using oversweep for deck parking. The horizontal tail surfaces also featured the same graceful curve on the leading edge as the glove box, the overall effect being rather similar to the Handley Page Victor.

Fuselage refinement
From the front the departures from AMSA 1968 were equally marked. Instead of a rather square-section fuselage flanked by squat double intakes, a more rounded fuselage flanked by thickish wing gloves with little sign of wing/body blending presented a more pleasing aspect, while the paired engines mounted in nacelles beneath the gloves showed side-by-side intakes instead of the previous horizontal split. With the

wing moved to the low position the engine nacelles formed a tunnel from which the main gear depended, unlike AMSA 1968, in which the main gear was retracted into the nacelles. This considerably reduced undercarriage track from 17.8ft (5.43m) to 12.1ft (3.69m), narrower than the ideal, but unavoidably so. The wings showed a slight anhedral, while the horizontal tail, mounted level with the wings, showed several degrees of dihedral.

The side elevation was much like that of the B-1 as we know it, except for the position of the horizontal tail, while the engine nacelles were considerably shorter than those on AMSA 1968, and featured a horizontal rather than a vertical rake to the inlets.

The Defense System Acquisition Review Council authorized full scale de-

velopment on June 4, 1970, and the contract awarded to Rockwell International was for five flight test and one static test aircraft. There was, however, a fly in the ointment: there simply was not enough money available, and Air Force approval to proceed with development was conditional on the project being tailored to suit the purse, so radical changes were inevitable. All the studies had assumed that the advanced avionics, defensive and offensive, would be made available, but in the event this was not the case. The requirements had been aimed far into the future, beyond immediate needs, and avionics development was halted, entirely through lack of funds. Instead, existing avionics were to be used, though provision was to be made for advanced equipment to be fitted at a later date.

Left: Defense Secretary Donald Rumsfeld prepares to board a B-1A at Edwards AFB on April 19, 1976. On landing after an hour-long flight during which he took a turn at the controls, former US Navy pilot and firm B-1 supporter Rumsfeld commented that the aircraft had handled "exceedingly well".

Right: In-flight refuelling was essential to the B-1A mission as originally envisaged and the first prototype is shown here conducting refuelling trials with a KC-135 tanker. The lines of the B-1 often belie its size, which can be judged here in comparison with the tanker.

After nearly nine years of the most careful studies and design work, it was ironic that the first major task after the contract had been awarded was to re-define the performance parameters and redesign the aircraft to fit the budget, a programme called Project Focus. The driving force was no longer cost effectiveness but cost limitation, a change of emphasis that was to have serious repercussions for the future, as it undermined the credibility of the B-1 in the eyes of the American public and, worse, the politicians.

It is a truism that in any field of endeavour the best is the enemy of the good; while there can be no doubt that the revised B-1 concept was very good indeed, it is equally certain that it was not as good as the original. Public and politicians naturally assumed that if the original aircraft was what was needed to fly the new mission successfully, the new and degraded version could not possibly have the necessary capability. Predictably, in view of the enormous cost, the project became a political football, though it still retained many supporters.

After avionics, the next area to come under close scrutiny was that of the structural materials used. The original design contained a high proportion of titanium (approximately 40 per cent of structural weight), and while titanium is a great weight saver compared to steel, it is also much more expensive. Rockwell were very experienced in the use of this material after building the XB-70 Valkyrie, and had developed a fabrication process known as diffusion bonding (described in detail in the following chapter) which gave great strength and was used in conjunction with welding and bolted joints. As well as saving weight – basically, the more titanium that can be substituted for steel, the greater the weight saved – titanium can also be used instead of aluminium in areas subject to aerodynamic heating, since it retains its strength in conditions where aluminium gradually weakens, such as flight at speeds exceeding Mach 2.2.

Both weight and cost in aircraft structures are very sensitive to the proportion of titanium used. Below about 12 per cent, in the specific case of the B-1, both cost and weight fall dramatically as the replacement of heavy steel sections with lighter titanium ones causes a knock-on effect through the design. Above this point, the weight continues to reduce while the cost levels out, until the proportion reaches 20 per cent, after which weight continues to diminish, albeit at a reduced rate, but costs start to spiral upward as many cheaper members are being replaced by the more expensive material. In the end, the proportion of titanium was reduced to about 21 per cent.

Materials specifications

Problems had arisen from the use of high strength steel alloys in the F-111, and the very long service life envisaged for the B-1 meant that this had to be avoided, so a requirement was added for the use of materials with superior fracture mechanics. In essence, this involved very strict manufacturing controls coupled with advances in non-destructive testing methods. It also involved the flaw size for a component being specified at an undetectable level; the component had then to be manufactured in such a way that the flaw could not become critical during the aircraft lifetime, which in the case of the B-1 was some 13,500 flying hours.

Project Focus had reduced the weapon load to 24 SRAMs instead of the 32 projected earlier, but design gross weight still increased from 350,870lb (159,155kg) to 360,000lb (163,296kg), and

the operational requirements were relaxed slightly. On paper these appear fairly marginal. The fully laden takeoff distance was extended by 500ft (152m); the supersonic dash distance was decreased by 100 statute miles (161km); the altitude for refuelling was reduced by 500ft (152m); and the thrust/drag ratio was reduced by about 10 per cent.

From Project Focus emerged the repackaged B-1, heavier but smaller, with length reduced to 143.5ft (43.74m), height to the top of the fin slightly increased at 32.4ft (9.88m), and span at minimum sweep reduced to 136.7ft (41.66m), while the wing gloves were smaller in span and no longer showed the graceful concave leading edge.

At the same time, two really major changes were apparent, the most obvious being the blending of the wing glove and the fuselage. This was adopted primarily to provide extra structural strength and extra volume while reducing the overall dimensions; it also helped to reduce the radar cross section (RCS) by smoothing out angles which would othewise have made excellent radar corners, though Rockwell staff remember this as more of a spinoff than a deliberate design feature.

The second major external change was the horizontal tail. That on the original proposal had been set low on the fuselage, roughly 5ft (1.52m) above the thrust line, where benefits in terms of both weight and stability were greatest, but in close proximity to the engine effluxes. The change from titanium to aluminium meant that the tailplane could not be exposed to such a demanding acoustic and temperature environment, and it was relocated halfway up the

vertical fin. Altered flutter characteristics made a complete redesign necessary, and the revised horizontal tail was of much more orthodox appearance than its predecessor. Although this increased the weight, it provided additional usable area in the tailcone for avionics.

A third, less obvious change concerned the engine intakes, The B-1 had two important flight regimes; Mach 2 at high altitude and low-level subsonic, and to provide the best solution to these

Above: The third B-1A transits the Mojave desert at about 500ft (150m). The fully swept wings notwithstanding, the power setting is only moderate. From this angle, the aircraft seems to be peering ahead.

Below: The third prototype during terrain following trials in September 1977 on its forty-eighth flight. The rear fuselage and the base of the fin are tufted.

Right: The third B-1A at medium altitude over one of the California dry lakes. The contrast with the T-38 chase aircraft gives an impression of size; the bomber's AoA is higher than that of the trainer.

Above: Condensation ripples from the trailing edge as the third B-1, seen here in polished natural metal, nears the contrail belt. Distinct vortices can be seen arising from the wing glove seal area.

Below: A slow pass with wings at minimum sweep by the third aircraft at Edwards. This could have been a minimum speed test but is probably a speed calibration check.

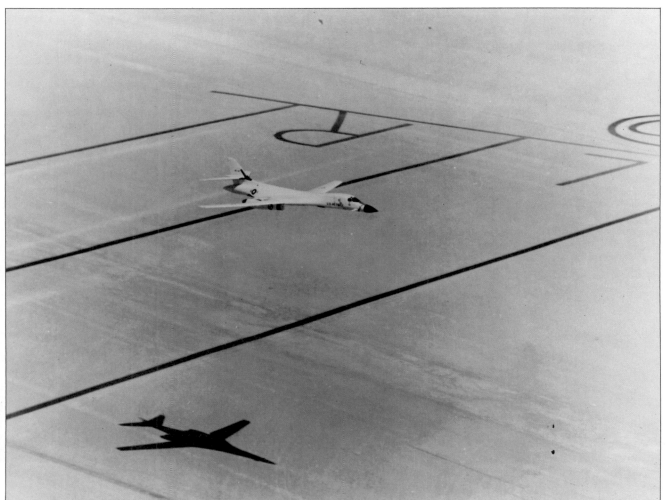

conflicting requirements a rather complex mixed compression intake had been adopted. Further studies showed that the use of a simple external compression intake would slightly enhance subsonic performance at the price of a corresponding restriction in the top right-hand corner of the performance envelope, but more than that, a weight saving of roughly 1,400lb (635kg) could be achieved.

By the middle of 1971 the basic configuration had stabilized, and in July of that year the Preliminary Design Review was held. This signalled the start of a new phase in which any changes would at the very least involve the preparation of new drawings, and in a worst case tooling and materials would have to be scrapped, an inevitably expensive process. Unfortunately further changes were unavoidable, as the emphasis on cost control had become even stronger than the previous stress on cost effec-

tiveness. In some cases it was found that the cost of a particular feature would be more than anticipated so that an alternative would have to be sought, the wing high-lift systems being a case in point. Originally these were conceived as double-slotted translating flaps, but the detail design soon showed that such a system would be both heavy and complicated, so an alternative was sought. A single slotted flap was designed and subjected to wind tunnel tests, which confirmed that it could meet the requirements. The leading edge slat was then extended inboard slightly, with the result that the high lift capability exceeded requirements.

Escape module revision

Another area subject to revision was the crew escape module. As first proposed it featured two rocket motors, one for primary propulsion and the other for manoeuvring, the latter being gimbal-mounted to allow manoeuvre in two axes. It was found that for a slight reduction in low-altitude adverse-attitude capability, one rocket motor, designed to give control in both roll and pitch, could do the job. The cost saving was considerable.

The contract placed with Rockwell on June 5, 1970, had been based on cost plus incentive fee and was planned on a series of milestones, at each of which approval had to be given before proceeding to the next phase. These were: (a) Preliminary design review of engines and avionics; (b) Mockup review; (c) Engine run to 90 per cent power; (d) Contract award for avionics integration; (e) Design review of engine; (f) Avionics mockup; (g) Engine preliminary flight rating test; (h) Rollout; (i) First flight; and (j) Production decision.

Unfortunately, inflation was beginning to bite, and cost overruns on other programmes, notably the C-5 Galaxy, were, raising fundamental questions

about procurement methods. Standard service practice before this time had been for the contractor to comply with the specification regardless of cost, but the first few months of the B-1 programme saw the USAF studying alternative methods. The result became known as the Innovative approach, with the head of the System Program Office, at that time Major-General Douglas Nelson, given a clear mandate to pull the basics of the programme together in such a way that costs would be reduced. In other contexts this would be known as horse trading.

The impact on the development programme was considerable. Two of the original five aircraft ordered for the flight test programme were eliminated, and the number of development engines was reduced from 40 to 27, while the target date for the first flight slipped by five months from December 1, 1973, to May 1, 1974. Worse still, the production decision, scheduled to be made six months after first flight, was deferred for a further six months, giving a total delay of 17 months. A high element of risk was attached to this programme, as it involved the lion's share of the flight test

programme being borne by the first prototype, so a serious mishap could have incalculable consequences.

Before the design finally settled down, a few minor changes took place. A radome replaced the tail cone, while a further, bullet-shaped sensor position appeared behind the junction of the vertical and horizontal tail surfaces. The overwing fairing was modified, as was the trailing edge fairing between the engine nozzles; the main landing gear strut was beefed up a bit; and the horizontal tail sweep angle was also modified. Span remained the same, but length showed a slight increase to 152.2ft (46.39m), as did overall height, to 33.58ft (10.23m). These were the final dimensions of the prototype B-1A.

The halting of the advanced avionics development caused a major headache, but with previous requirements as a guide, a package of existing sub-systems was put together. The big question mark against advanced systems is always whether they are going to work as advertised, whereas with existing equipment the reverse is the case: the question then is, in a long-term programme, are the items still going to be

manufactured and available when they are wanted? The uncertainty was aggravated by the long service life envisaged for the B-1. Naturally, mid-life updates were anticipated, but it could just turn out that a particular item would perform well enough to be retained, and might well be wanted 30 years in the future. If it was ten years old to start with...?

Avionics selection

The package selected consisted of such systems as a stellar-inertial navigation platform, forward-looking and terrain-following radar, radar altimeter and other items combined with a central computer complex. Examination deemed the computer complex risky and expensive; consequently, a modified off-the-shelf computer was substituted. At this point the avionics were split into two packages, offensive and defensive, and defensive systems were recategorized to allow open competition in order to reduce the risks, both technical and fiscal. In April 1972 Boeing was selected to integrate the offensive avionic systems, and after a period of intensive evaluation the AIL Division of Cutler-

Hammer secured the order to do the same job on the defensive avionic systems. This award was made in January 1974, barely four months before the first flight was scheduled to take place, but by this time the programme had slipped a few months.

In 1973, construction started of the first B-1 prototype, and even as this happened further ventures to improve later variants or to upgrade standard models were under review. Many of these were in the field of avionics, and one improvement that did get through in the end was a new, cheap, but highly accurate inertial navigation platform, but there were some other very interesting ideas which seem to have been all but forgotten in the years since 1973. One was a new wing carry-through box by Advanced Metallic Structures. Two concepts were evaluated and one was to be constructed and tested, the design conforming to the

B-1A fourth prototype (76-0174)

The first B-1 to wear camouflage, 76-0174 also carried a dorsal spine housing a waveguide for a monopulse jamming system called Cross-Eye.

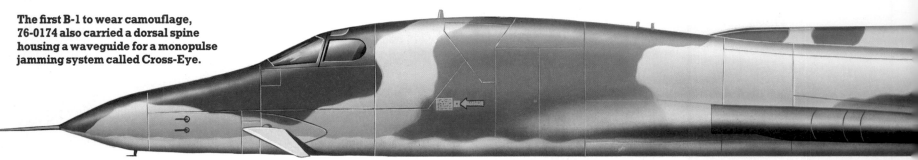

Above: The dorsal spine on B-1A No 4 is clearly shown. This was not featured on any other aircraft and does not appear on every picture of this one. Also highlighted is the original wing seal fairing.

dimensions and structural needs of the B-1. Little has ever been released, except that the use of advanced materials and concepts was expected to produce large savings in both weight and cost, and it might be incorporated into later B-1s on the production line.

The other possibility was the supercritical wing, at that time about to be flown on the F-111, which was designed to offer higher cruising speeds, simpler construction and, almost certainly, reduced costs. To retrofit the supercritical wing is a fairly easy job with a variable-sweep aircraft, and might have been done as a mid-life update, but little has since been heard of the programme, and its use for the B-1 has long since been shelved.

As if the impact of the so-called Innovative approach had not been bad enough, the programme schedule was disrupted yet again in July 1973 by the

USAF's new fly-before-buy policy. This slowed progress up still further, with the projected date for first flight being delayed several months; even worse, from a production point of view, was that the time between first flight and the decision to commence production was doubled from 12 to 24 months. This was difficult for Rockwell. The third prototype would be completed early in 1976, after which manufacturing would grind to a halt; then, if the decision proved favourable, it would have to restart at the end of the year. At this stage some 3,000 suppliers and subcontractors were involved in the project, and the task of rescheduling that lot, as well as finding interim work for many thousands of direct employees, was no joke. Once skilled workers are laid off, getting them back in times of full employment is not easy

By this time the US Senate Armed Services Research and Development Subcommittee was growing worried about the situation. In the late summer of 1973 Air Force Secretary John L. McLucas ordered an independent review, headed by Raymond Bisplinghoff, at that time the Deputy Director of the National Science Foundation. The report

Above: No 4 before the application of camouflage and without the dorsal spine. The black dielectric panels on the wing glove roots accentuate the waisted effect of the central fuselage.

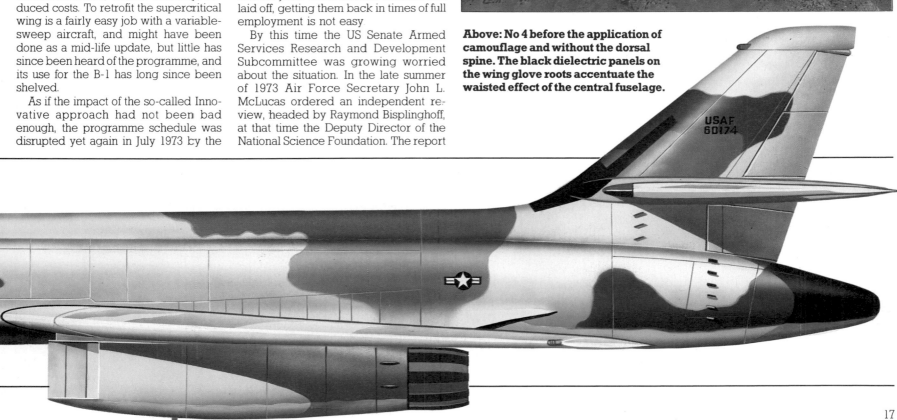

produced by Bisplinghoff's team of technical and management experts was critical of the development programme in a number of areas, but particularly the cheeseparing environment.

While the report's conclusions were largely ignored, it is worth examining the salient points in order to appreciate the difficulties under which the project operated. Firstly, the programme was so totally success-oriented yet so austerely funded that it would be difficult to switch over from development to full scale production. Secondly, three prototypes were inadequate for the development of such a complex design. Thirdly, the

rephased development programme would cause both delays and extra costs, estimated as not less than $300 million. Fourthly, insufficient funding was available to ensure programme flexibility. Fifthly, the flight test programme envisaged would be "minimal", and heavily dependent upon the first prototype for at least the first year. And finally, several technical and design aspects were criticized, among them the overwing fairing and the electrical multiplex system.

The USAF agreed with almost all these points, but stated that they arose largely from budgetary constraints, so contractor management procedures

were tightened up after the preliminary report, and it was agreed to try and fund a fourth prototype. The only reason that the project had not been terminated was the absolute belief that the B-1 would be vital to the security of the United States.

Development and design refinement remained a dynamic process throughout this period. One of the suggested changes was to eliminate the variable-sweep wing, thereby saving weight and complexity, and to fix the wing at an angle of 50°. This would have been self-defeating in terms of the mission requirements, and the B-1½, as it was mockingly called, was returned to the closet.

Above: A busy scene at Edwards, with all four B-1As under one roof. Seen clockwise from the left are No 2, with the aft radome open; No 4; No 1; and No 3, seen here with starboard wing spoilers extended.

One major change stemming from test results, which found the crew capsule to be unstable at speeds above 300kt (556km/hr), came in October 1974, when the decision was taken to revert to ejection seats for the four crew members. If the two instructors were carried, they would be forced to leave the aircraft through the belly hatch. The first three

B-1 cruise missile carrier proposal

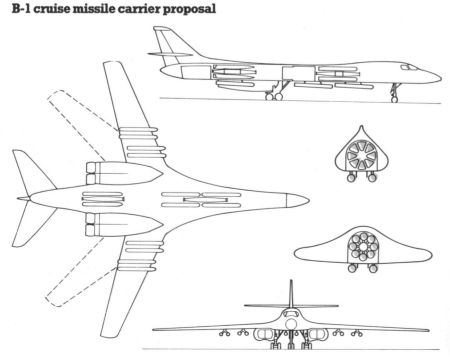

Left: In the wake of the programme's cancellation in 1977, Rockwell proposed this fixed-wing version of the B-1 optimized for internal and external carriage of 30 Tomahawk or ALCM cruise missiles.

Below: Boeing proposed a 747-200F for the stand-off missile launcher role, with a payload of between 70 and 90 weapons. ALCMs were to be carried internally and launched through a side door at the rear.

B-1 core aircraft proposal

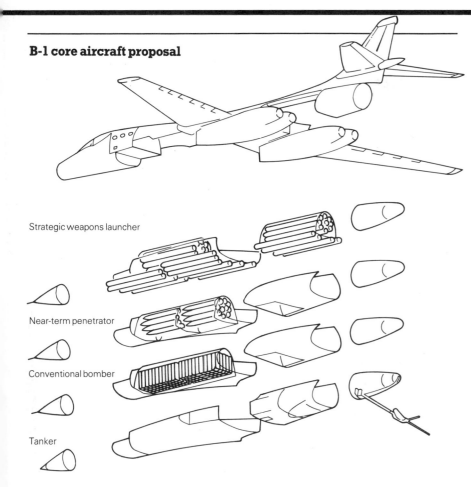

Strategic weapons launcher

Near-term penetrator

Conventional bomber

Tanker

By 1979 Rockwell had produced this scheme for a family of aircraft based on the B-1 and adaptable to various roles. The wings were to be fixed at a 25° sweep angle and limiting the aircraft to subsonic speeds would enable the percentage of titanium to be reduced to 8 per cent: along with other changes, these would allow the cost per aircraft to be reduced by more than one third. The strategic weapons launcher would carry up to 30 cruise missiles; the near-term penetrator

would accommodate two eight-round SRAM launchers and a fuel tank, bridging the gap between the B-52 and the next generation of bombers; the conventional bomber would replace the penetrator's SRAMs with bombs, mines or Harpoon missiles; and the tanker would have a fuel tank module forward with more fuel and a boom operator's compartment aft; in each case a nose radome and tail equipment bay appropriate to the mission would be carried.

prototypes were too far along the manufacturing process to be altered, but aircraft No. 4 and all subsequent models would have ejection seats. The maximum weight had also crept up to 395,000lb (179,172kg).

The first B-1 was rolled out at Palmdale, California, on October 26, 1974, at a ceremony presided over by Defense Secretary Dr. James R. Schlesinger. In his speech, he commented: "Deterrence, it is said, lies in the eye of the beholder. It works by acting on the psychology, on attitudes, and the perceptions of difficulties recognized by the potential attacker. In this respect, the bomber is unique: there is no satisfactory substitute for its contribution to that overall panoply of forces which achieve deterrence.' He also sounded a warning note. "A prerequisite for any affirmative decision [on production] is that the B-1 continues to perform throughout the entire Research and Development sequence in a manner that is highly acceptable."

After extensive ground checks the first B-1, 74-0158, left the ground at Palmdale on December 23, 1974, and after a flight lasting 78 minutes, it landed at Edwards Air Force Base. There were no untoward incidents, and the aircraft, the flying qualities test vehicle, immediately began its allotted test programme.

At this point more than 20,000 hours of wind tunnel testing had gone into the project, the final effort being full scale tests to verify that the engines were compatible with the intakes. Predicted lift/drag ratios, stability and control over the entire gamut of flight conditions had all been checked out. Now the proving time had come, with the start of what would later be described as "probably the most successful flight test programme of all time." (This was an Air

Force comment, not manufacturer's hype.)

As originally planned, the flight test programme was to start with clearance for low-level flight at speeds up to Mach 0.85, with a minimum of 18 flights to be made in the first six months. In spite of using telemetry for in-flight data transmission, the factor determining progress would be the rate at which the data from each flight could be analyzed and processed. In-flight refuelling was to be used to extend mission time where practicable, and this was particularly valuable for flutter testing at maximum weight, as the aircraft did not need to land to top up with fuel to bring the weight back up to the required level.

As it proceeded, the test programme deviated somewhat from that originally planned. There is obviously some risk in low flying, and with only one flight test aircraft available for some time, a more cautious course was adopted, with the flight envelope only gradually explored. Both in the air and on the ground, further milestones in the development programme were passed, and April 10, 1975, was notable for two: the first supersonic flight was made, a speed of Mach 1.05 being reached; and on the same mission in-flight refuelling was used for the first time. Meanwhile, the second development aircraft, No. 74-0159, was undergoing the full-scale static/strength and proof loading tests. These were conducted at Palmdale by the Lockheed Aircraft Corporation and were completed during July of that year.

Right: Flight testing continued after 1977, with the fourth prototype concentrating on evaluation of its ability to use its defensive systems to penetrate hostile airspace.

The next event was particularly momentous: Rockwell were awarded a contract for a fourth B-1. In line with previous decisions, this would have ejection seats, a redesigned forward fuselage with the crew capsule deleted, revised engine nacelles and a bay aft to accommodate defensive avionics.

Low-level flight testing began in earnest on September 19, 1975, when the first, and still the only flying B-1 reached Mach 0.75 at 500ft (152m), over the Pacific test range. The limits were gradually pushed faster and lower until, on November 11, speeds ranging from 165kt (306km/h) to a maximum of Mach 0.83 – roughly 550kt (1,020km/h) – were demonstrated over the main runway at Edwards at an altitude of 200ft (61m).

Second to fly

The burden of the entire flight test programme was carried by the first B-1 for a total of 15 months before it was joined by the third development aircraft. No 74-0160 was rolled out on January 16, 1976, and made its first flight on April 1, and the arrival of this aircraft, scheduled for offensive avionics, terrain-following, and weapons delivery trials, must have occasioned a huge sigh of relief among those closely concerned with the programme. It was quickly joined by the second B-1, No. 74-0159, which, its loading test function completed, had been put back into flying order. It was rolled out on May 11, and made its first flight on June 14.

With three B-1s flying, the test programme proceeded apace, and the Initial Operational Test and Evaluation (IOTE) flights, which were simulated Strategic Air Command missions, were successfully completed in September of that year. These were followed on December 1 by the completion of DSARC III, the production decision: including those already existing, a total of 244 B-1 bombers would be procured.

After all the trials, tribulations and general abuse, including the appellation B-1 Bummer that the project had suffered during its long and penurious life, it now seemed to be riding the crest of a wave. This feeling was reinforced in April 1977, when the entire B-1 team, both civil and military, was awarded the prestigious Collier Trophy, presented annually for "The greatest achievement in aeronautics or astronautics in America, in respect of improving the performance, efficiency, or safety, of air or space vehicles." At this point, the 100th test mission had just been flown. Taken by the third B-1 on March 29, it had covered over-water navigation and terrain-following tests and simulated SRAM missile release. The 34th flight by this aircraft, it brought total flight hours to 542.

But already the storm clouds were gathering, and in March a Pentagon study had proposed that the total number of B-1s be cut to 150. Arms reduction negotiations with the Soviet Union were in progress at the time, and President Carter had retained the option to delete the B-1 entirely if satisfactory progress was made towards disarmament. Then, in May, it was revealed that the unit cost of the aircraft would top $100 million. This caused a furore among the opponents of the B-1, to put it mildly, and even gave many moderates pause for thought. Once again, the project begun all those years and all those dollars ago was teetering on the brink of disaster.

The axe fell on June 30, when President Carter announced the he would not approve production of the B-1. His decision was made on the recommendation of Defense Secretary Harold Brown, who later defended the Pentagon's reasoning in the following terms: "My recommendation to the President... [was] based on the conclusion that aircraft carrying modern cruise missiles will better assure the effectiveness of the bomber component of US strategic forces in the 1980s... I concluded that on the basis of new design features resulting from progress in cruise missile technology, and in the light of proven test results, the assurance of successful operation of the cruise missile against future Soviet defences is now very high. I further concluded that ... the cruise missile options offer more certainty of high effectiveness. Moreover, the cruise missile option is less expensive." The carrier for the new weapon was to be the already elderly B-52, and another acronym nearly joined the already long list in the B-1 story: MROOBA (Must Refurbish Our Old Bombers Again).

Immediately following the President's announcement, the Air Force imposed a 90-day stop order on B-1 production, pending the termination, which came on July 6, of all B-1 production contracts by the Defense Secretary. The only gleam of light remained in the fact that the existing aircraft were to be retained for a research and development programme, and that the fourth B-1, at the time about 45 per cent complete and slated to develop the full avionic system capability, was not affected by the stop order. The first production aircraft, Nos 5, 6 and 7, which had already been started, were halted.

Termination of the programme was a heavy blow to Rockwell International. Over 8,000 workers had to be laid off, and many others redeployed, though the nucleus of the team was kept together by seeking subcontract work wherever it could be obtained – from Boeing on 747 and 757 airliners, from Airbus Industrie, from British Aerospace and so on. The engineering team was subcontracted out to whoever needed it for periods varying between six months and three years while remaining on Rockwell's payroll; in this way it generated turn-

over, as it was hired out on a cost plus basis, while being kept together; without it, Rockwell could have been out of the big league for good. A spin-off benefit was that the engineers were kept current on technology.

Less than two weeks after cancellation of the B-1A, Rockwell began submitting proposals for R&D programmes to the Air Force, which in turn submitted a restructured programme for B-1 development to the Defense Secretary on October 7. The outcome was the Bomber Penetration Evaluation (BPE), which was to last until January 1981, and during which the B-1 gained five new acronyms: NTP (Near Term Penetrator), SWL (Strategic Weapons Launcher), CMCA (Cruise Missile Carrier Aircraft), MRB (Multi Role Bomber), and finally LRCA (Long Range Combat Aircraft). The NTP was intended as an interim bomber to bridge the gap between the B-52 and something better than the B-1; otherwise the descriptions are self-explanatory.

Relegated to research

Once again the B-1 took to the skies, although now relegated to the role of a research vehicle, in an exhaustive programme that was, although nobody realised it at the time, to involve more than 1,350 flying hours and last some three and a half years.

On October 5, 1978, the second prototype attained its highest ever speed of Mach 2.22 at an altitude of 50,000ft (15,240m). The programme was further augmented on February 14, 1979, when the fourth B-1, No. 76-0174, made its maiden flight from Palmdale to Edwards. This was the full capability aircraft, so avionic systems testing could now begin in earnest. This aircraft was slightly different in appearance from its predecessors in that it featured a dorsal spine

housing some temporary test equipment for the avionic suites. Much of its flight time was taken up in comprehensive test sorties in a Red Flag environment, to evaluate how well it performed against both American and simulated Soviet

Above: The mission profile of the B-1 includes a subsonic cruise at high altitude to conserve fuel while in friendly or neutral airspace. This is its natural habitat on the outbound and homeward legs.

Below: The second B-1A, seen here on March 23, 1983, the day it initiated the B-1B flight test programme. The modifications carried out during the previous nine months resulted in few external changes.

B-1A second prototype

74-0159 resplendent in the livery of the B-1B test programme. Widely hailed as the first B-1B, it was really only a modified B-1A.

U.S. AIR FORCE

In the early days of the B-1A its radar cross section had been quoted as anything between 1/35 and 1/25 that of the B-52. The BPE had shown just how important low observability was in aiding penetration; countermeasures were valuable, but were emissions that might prove counter-productive by giving away the position, or at least the presence, of the aircraft.

On December 2 General Mathis, Vice Chief of Staff of the Air Force, issued a letter formally designating the new strategic bomber proposal the LRCA; six days later it was decided to extend BPE flight testing through April 1981. By the beginning of 1980 new-generations of offensive and defensive avionics were being used in the tests, which still concentrated on airborne controlled interception. (Although never officially stated, it was obvious that the interceptor fighter was regarded as the main threat.)

BPE completion
The final flight test in the BPE, flown by the fourth B-1A on April 29, 1981, concluded all B-1 test flying; since the first flight in December 1974 a total of 1,895.2 flight hours had been accumulated, shared among the four prototypes as follows:

No 1: 79 missions, 405.3 hours
No 2: 60 missions, 282.5 hours
No 3: 138 missions, 829.4 hours
No 4: 70 missions, 378 hours

In addition more than 25,000 hours of wind tunnel testing had taken place, the engines had accumulated nearly 7,600 flight hours, and the structural article had been subjected to fatigue testing designed to simulate three aircraft lifetimes, while weapons tests had included the dropping of some 45 B-61 inert nuclear weapons and the air launching of two SRAMs.

On April 7 the Bomber Alternatives Study Interim Report had been submitted to Congress, and June 4 saw the completion of the Manned Bomber Penetrativity Evaluation Flight Test Results and Report by the Air Force Test and Evaluation Center at Edwards AFB. The contenders were the refurbished B-52, equipped with updated electronics; an extensively modified FB-111 – the FB-IIIH – a cheap but definitely interim solution with longer range than the standard version but no ALCM carrying capability; a jumbo jet type modified to carry a heavy load of ALCMs; and the B-1 modified for greater range, a heavier and much more diverse payload, and lower observability, traded

Above: The underside of 74-0159 showing the modified weapons bay doors. Some extra dielectric panels have appeared, but most of the other modifications carried out are not readily apparent.

Below: In-flight refuelling is not necessarily a straight and level process, but must occasionally be carried out in a turn, as this picture shows. Despite its size, the B-1 is easy to fly accurately.

defensive systems, a task in which it was aided by the third prototype.

The BPE dragged along on a hand-to-mouth basis, never quite knowing when it might be terminated. The first reprieve came in October 1979, when Congress appropriated funds to continue the evaluation of operational penetration techniques and the defensive avionics, and was followed on January 29, 1980, by an official extension of the BPE to June 30, 1981, although the flight test programme would be completed long before then. It

was also planned to convert the third B-1 to carry Air-Launched Cruise Missiles (ALCMs) both in the internal weapons bays and on pylons externally, while the fourth aircraft continued to fly against various radars and missile defences until October 27, when the decision was taken to concentrate on Airborne Controlled Intercepts.

Meanwhile, behind the scenes the pot was once again coming to the boil. Yet another study group had been set up on August 22 to evaluate bomber alternatives, headed by Dr. Zeiberg of the Office of the Secretary of Defense and divided into five panels covering mission and requirements, the threat, aircraft system design, planning and programme, and systems evaluation. The consideration of low observables is conspicuous by its absence, since it was becoming clear that stealth technology was of primary importance in the penetration missions: indeed, the existence of such a programme was sprung on the unsuspecting nation just three days later by Defense Secretary Harold Brown, when he announced a research programme into the subject as the basis of an advanced technology project for the future.

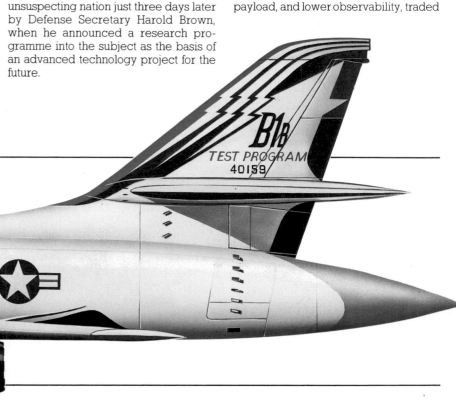

Above: The first production B-1B taxies out at Edwards AFB in October 1984. The small transparency added to the avionics operator's station is just visible, while the shadow of the wing betrays the slat detail.

Below: August 1984, and 74-0159 demonstrates its short takeoff roll at Edwards. Compare the tailcone and fin fairing with those of the aircraft pictured above: the B-1A's are pointed whereas on the B-1B they are blunt.

Bottom: 74-0159 leaves the Edwards runway, with the new dark paint scheme giving it a menacing aspect. It is noteworthy that even the engine intakes are dark rather than the more usual white.

against the Mach 2 capability, which was by this time looking a handicap rather than an asset.

The B-52 was not immortal, but at this time it was judged still capable of carrying out the penetration mission at least until the late 1980s. The Advanced Technology Bomber (ATB), still a dream of the future, could not be certain within the required timescale, and should the B-52 be selected for further service life extension there would still be a gap in penetration ability from about 1987 to 1995. The modified FB-111 was attractive from a cost standpoint, but while its penetration capability was undoubted, its inability to carry a heavy enough payload told against it; a buy of about 150 was contemplated, but they would have been inadequate for the task. The large cruise missile carrier was always an outsider in the contest: it would have been limited in every respect apart from weapon load, since it lacked dispersal capability and mission flexibility.

Against these options, the B-1B, beefed up to carry an extra 82,000lb (37,195kg) of payload, with a longer range and lower radar signature than the B-1A, plus a flight proven airframe and engines, looked a very good bet indeed. The report had concluded that the next strategic bomber should be capable of fulfilling requirements additional to the nuclear strike role – basically the iron bomb mission, maritime patrol, and minelaying – and that the B-1 derivative was the best option within the projected need for an Initial Operational Capability (IOC) by 1986.

It was becoming obvious that the United States needed a new long range multirole aircraft and that the B-1B was the only real contender, a fact confirmed on October 2, 1981, when President Reagan announced the decision to build 100 B-1Bs to have an IOC some time in 1986. This would coincide with the predicted inability of the B-52 to carry out the low-level penetration mission, leaving the surviving B-52s to carry out the less demanding role of stand-off cruise missile carriers. In the meantime, the ATB, or stealth bomber, could be developed in a less urgent atmosphere.

President Reagan's announcement was followed in November by a joint letter to Congress from Defense Secret-

Above: Flaps and slats extended and a touch of right rudder as 74-0159 lines up on the runway. This shot was taken just 12 days before the aircraft's fatal accident, which occurred during a test flight on August 29, 1984.

Below: Farnborough 82, and 76-0174 joins the static display after flying non-stop from California. The dorsal spine, blunt tailcone and camouflage scheme are the distinguishing features of this aircraft.

ary Caspar Weinberger and the Director of the CIA, confirming that the B-1B would be able to penetrate the projected Soviet defences until well into the 1990s, and in December the Senate approved full funding. The total cost of the B-1B procurment programme had been fixed at $20.5 billion calculated at Fiscal Year 1981 rates.

Contracts awarded

1982 might well be described as the year of the contract. Full scale development and Lot 1 production was awarded to Rockwell on January 20; the first batch of engines was ordered from General Electric on April 1; the AIL Division of Eaton Corporation (formerly Cutler Hammer) received the order for Lot 1 of the defensive avionics on June 8; and just three days later the offensive avionic suite Lot 1 was awarded to the Boeing Military Airplane Company. Also in June the initial review for the B-1B was completed.

At this point, of course, the B-1B did not exist, though tremendous effort had gone into making the B-1A – the only available hardware – a multirole aircraft. The vast increase in payload had to be achieved at little or no cost in structural weight, despite the obvious necessity to beef up the undercarriage to carry the increased gross weight at takeoff, and was to be achieved by a weight trimming programme. Some weight could be saved by trading off the Mach 2 capability, and more by revising the wing seals, while improved aerodynamic efficiency would also help. At the same time, to increase penetration capability, and with it mission survivability, the avionics suites

were to be upgraded using off-the-shelf products as far as possible.

One suggestion which was not adopted was to limit the wing sweep angle to a maximum angle of 60°. As the wings transitioned, they caused changes in the aircraft centre of gravity, which was compensated for automatically by the transfer of fuel between various internal tanks. A simplified system could have saved weight, but would have reduced the excellent low-level ride qualities as it increased aspect ratio.

A new 1,100-hour flight test programme was planned: the first and third aircraft, which had the highest time, were to be stored and subsequently cannibalized for spares, and the new programme was built around the two low-time B-1As, the second and fourth prototypes. Production B-1Bs were also scheduled to join the programme as various later stages were reached. Meanwhile, the flying ceased as the Air Force and Rockwell sorted out exactly what they were going to do. The fourth B-1A made a brief excursion across the Atlantic in September 1982 to the Farnborough Air Show, during which it clocked up a further 28 flying hours; it was then grounded for avionics modifications, and was not to fly again before the summer of 1984.

During the summer of 1982 work started on the second prototype to modify it for the B-1B programme. Changes included new weapons bay doors and modifications to some bulkheads and the flight control systems. It was originally anticipated that this work would take about 21 months, but in the event the aircraft was flying again on

March 23, 1983, just nine months later. Its test functions were to cover stability and control, flutter, and weapons release, and although it was widely hailed by the Press as the first B-1B, it was actually just a modified B-1A. Once again the flight test programme depended on a single aircraft for a protracted period, but at least this time it was a flight-proven aircraft.

The fourth B-1A rejoined the test programme with a flight on July 30, 1984. Equipped with new avionic systems, both defensive and offensive, it was scheduled to fly some 380 hours in the next phase, and some idea of the rate of progress is given by the fact that during the next nine months it flew 24 missions, totalling 120 hours. The accent was on testing the defensive avionic systems first before switching to full system clearance. Meanwhile, the second prototype has been making good progress, and was only four flights away from concluding its allotted programme when, on August 29, 1984, it crashed, killing the chief test pilot of Rockwell International, Doug Benefield, and seriously injuring the other crew members.

This fateful flight was, until the unfortunate accident, quite routine. The original flight plan called for takeoff at 06.30 hours and a duration of 4 hours 20 minutes; takeoff was to be at a 9° pitch attitude, followed by airspeed calibration tests in the Edwards tower flyby pattern, then static and dynamic minimum speed control tests in the Cords Road area. After refuelling in flight, the aircraft would head for the Edwards Precision Impact Range Area (PIRA), where it was to make to weapons release

passes, the first simulated, and the second releasing five Mk 82 high-drag bombs whose warheads were filled with concrete.

The mission would end with touch-and-go landings back at Edwards with Doug Benefield acting as instructor pilot to the command pilot, Major Richard V. Reynolds; 69 days had elapsed since Major Reynolds had made a landing in the B-1, whereas to remain current on type a landing is required every 60 days (in all other aspects of flying the B-1 Major Reynolds was current). The final point was a landing touchdown load test followed by a full stopping test on maximum braking effectiveness.

The engines were started at 05.43, and the big bomber began to taxi out at 06.18. During the taxiing phase ground load survey turning tests were carried out on the ramp, after which the aircraft proceeded to Runway 22, where a final pre-flight check revealed that scuffing during the turning tests had caused excessive wear to both nose gear tyres, and tyres 3 and 8 on the main gear. The aircraft then returned to the ramp for remedial work, completed by approximately 08.30.

Edwards AFB is one of the busiest in the world, and the delay, caused by a trifling matter, meant that the order of the mission had to be rescheduled so as to

avoid disruption of other activities planned for that day. The revised test sequence was now: takeoff; weapons release; airspeed calibration; minimum speed control; and landing. The first two phases were uneventful, though the air-speed calibration tests were curtailed after two passes due to thermal turbulence threatening to make the data obtained invalid.

At 10.12, some 43 minutes after takeoff, the B-1, accompanied by its F-111 chase aircraft, climbed to 6,000ft (1,830m) in the Cords Road area, and was configured for the static minimum control speed points,

with wing sweep at 55°, flaps, slats and gear retracted, and the centre of gravity at 45 per cent of Mean Aerodynamic Chord (MAC). This test was successfully carried out at a speed of about 250kt (463km/h). Normally the centre of gravity changes would be carried out auto-

Below: The first production B-1B, 82-0001, inaugurates a new chapter in the long and tortuous story of Strategic Air Command's new bomber. Having just taken off from Palmdale on its maiden flight, it passes overhead en route to Edwards AFB.

Below: The first production B-1B in Rockwell's vast checkout facility at Palmdale, which can accommodate four aircraft at a time. Behind the aircraft is one of the control rooms for the test engineers; around three-quarters of the tests have been automated.

matically, but the nature of this test series called for manual operation.

The next test was dynamic minimum control speed, with the wings fully extended at 15°, flaps, slats, and landing gear all down, the centre of gravity at the aft limit for that configuration of 21 per

Below: 82-0001 at the moment of lift off from Palmdale, on its way to join the fourth B-1A in the flight test programme at Edwards. Camouflage details are more clearly shown in this picture than most – note the tiny star and bar marking.

cent MAC, and a speed of 138kt (256km/h). The B-1A accelerated to 300kt (556km/h), whereupon sweeping the wings commenced, a process that took 46 seconds. The flaps, slats and landing gear were all extended, but the centre of gravity was left unchanged, far outside the limit for that particular configuration, and as the airspeed decayed through 145kt (269km/h), with the angle of incidence rising to 8.5°, the aircraft suffered an uncontrollable pitch-up to an angle of 70°. Despite the application of full forward stick and left rudder, the aircraft was in an irrecoverable position,

and Major Reynolds intitiated the ejection procedure.

Even now all should have been well for the crew. This aircraft was one of the original three with the crew escape module which had been designed to separate at low altitudes and adverse attitudes, correct its attitude and regain sufficient height for the parachutes to deploy, then make a soft landing on the impact bladders. However, one of the explosive repositioning bolts failed to function, and the module made a hard nose-down landing, with tragic results.

The main finding of the accident in-

vestigation board was as follows. "There was deviation from flight manual procedures in that the wings were brought forward without either resetting the CG control panel from 45 to 21 per cent (21 per cent was the minimum for that particular configuration) MAC or checking that the CG was within limits before sweeping the wings. This resulted in the aircraft exceeding the aft CG limits as defined in the flight manual."

Meanwhile, back at Palmdale, an exciting event was about to take place: the rollout of the first production aircraft, a genuine B-1B, on September 4, 1984. On October 18 it made its maiden flight to Edwards, to join the test programme as a full capability aircraft. Much more development lay ahead – even when this book appears it will not be complete – but 23 years after the initiation of the first exploratory studies by the USAF, a production bomber had appeared, to enter service within a year, and to achieve IOC within two years,

This was indeed a milestone. An earlier loss of the second prototype might have proved much more serious, but as it was, although tragic, it did nothing to further hurt or delay the programme. The first B-1B, No. 82-0001, was to join the fourth prototype, and the work slated for the lost prototype was taken over by the ninth production aircraft.

Below: July 27, 1985, and Air Force Secretary Verne Orr formally hands over the first operational B-1B to General Bennie L. Davis, Commander in Chief of Strategic Air Command, at Offutt AFB, Nebraska, the command's HQ. This is the second production aircraft, serial number 83-0065.

Structure

Conflicting requirements for rapid start-up and getaway, the use of short runways and austere airfields, Mach 2 at high altitudes and extended penetration at high subsonic speeds at low levels, and very heavy payloads and intercontinental range, made the use of a variable-sweep wing for the B-1 almost inevitable. At the same time, the decision to carry the payload and fuel internally, although later amended, placed a premium on available volume, leading to wing/body blending and in turn reducing radar signature. The reduction in radar signature, in fact, was so marked that much further effort was concentrated on this aspect, especially for the B-1B, even to the extent of dropping the Mach 2 requirement.

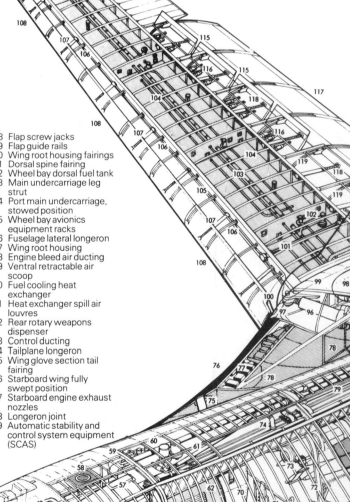

The B-1's main fuselage is a traditional monocoque, with frames, skins and longerons forming a cohesive whole, although to make maintenance easier as many as possible of the load carrying paths are internal, thus reducing the number of external structural panels. The internal structure is very concentrated, with frames spaced at roughly 10in (250mm) intervals for the entire length of the fuselage.

The fuselage is manufactured in sections, and these are assembled first, before the wings, undercarriage, engine

nacelles and empennage are attached. The forward fuselage section contains the radome, the radar avionics bay, the nose gear bay which is beneath the crew compartment, the environmental equipment bay, a section of the forward fuel tank, and most of the avionics bays, which fill almost the entire cross-section of the fuselage just astern of the crew compartment. Next comes the forward intermediate section, which contains the front and intermediate weapons bays, with integral fuel tanks to each side.

The wing/body blending begins here.

As previously related, this was adopted for many reasons, among which were the need to increase strength and volume. It reduced structural weight by more than 5 per cent and slightly reduced transonic drag without increasing subsonic and supersonic drag. Yet another advantage lay in the amount of body lift generated – about 50 per cent in the high-speed low-

altitude regime – while the additional fuel housed would otherwise have occupied some weapons bay volume. More avionics are also sited in this area. Behind the front intermediate fuselage section comes the massive titanium wing carry-through (WCT) box, which also serves as an integral fuel tank.

Astern of the WCT box, the aft intermediate fuselage section houses the main gear well, with a fuel tank above it, and a flight controls mixer compartment. Further avionics are accommodated in a 14in (35m) wide compartment between

Rockwell International B-1B cutaway

1 Radome
2 Multi-mode phased array radar scanner
3 Low-observable shrouded scanner tracking mechanism
4 Radar mounting bulkhead
5 Radome hinge joint
6 In-flight refuelling receptacle, open
7 Nose avionics equipment bays
8 APQ-164 offensive radar system
9 Dual pitot heads
10 Foreplane hydraulic actuator
11 Structural mode control system (SMCS) ride control foreplane
12 Foreplane pivot fixing
13 Front pressure bulkhead
14 Nose undercarriage wheel bay
15 Nosewheel doors
16 Control cable runs
17 Cockpit floor level
18 Rudder pedals
19 Control column, quadruplex automatic flight control system
20 Instrument panel shroud
21 Windscreen panels
22 Detachable nuclear flash screens, all window positions
23 Co-pilot's ejection seat
24 Co-pilot's emergency escape hatch
25 Overhead switch panel
26 Pilot's emergency escape hatch
27 Cockpit eyebrow window
28 Ejection seat launch/ mounting rails
29 Pilot's Weber ACES 'zero-zero' ejection seat
30 Wing sweep control lever
31 Cockpit section framing
32 Toilet
33 Nose undercarriage drag brace
34 Twin landing lamps
35 Taxiing lamp
36 Shock absorber strut
37 Twin nosewheels, forward retracting
38 Torque scissor links
39 Hydraulic steering control unit
40 Nosewheel leg door
41 Retractable boarding ladder
42 Ventral crew entry hatch, open
43 Nose undercarriage pivot fixing
44 Hydraulic retraction jack
45 Systems Operators' instrument console
46 Radar hand controller
47 Crew cabin side window panel
48 Offensive Systems Operators' ejection seat (OSO)
49 Cabin roof escape hatches

50 Defensive Systems Operator's ejection seat (DSO)
51 Rear pressure bulkhead
52 External emergency release handle
53 Underfloor air conditioning ducting
54 Air system ground connection
55 External access panels
56 Avionics equipment racks, port and starboard
57 Cooling air exhaust duct
58 Astro navigation antenna
59 Forward fuselage joint frame
60 Air system valves and ducting
61 Dorsal systems and equipment duct
62 Weapons bay extended range fuel tank
63 Electrical cable multiplexes
64 Forward fuselage integral fuel tank
65 Electronics equipment bay
66 Ground cooling air connection
67 Defensive avionics system transmitting antennas
68 Weapons bay door hinge mechanism
69 Forward weapons bay
70 Weapons bay doors, open
71 Retractable spoiler
72 Movable (non-structural) weapons bay bulkhead to suit varying load sizes
73 Rotary dispenser hydraulic drive motor
74 Fuel system piping
75 Communications antennas, port and starboard
76 Starboard lateral radome
77 ALQ-161 defensive avionics system equipment
78 Forward fuselage fuel tanks
79 Control cable runs
80 Rotary weapons dispenser
81 AGM-69 SRAM short-range air-to-surface missiles
82 Weapons bay door and hinge links
83 Port defensive avionics system equipment

84 Fuselage flank fuel tanks
85 Defensive avionics system transmitting antennas
86 Port lateral radome
87 Port navigation light
88 Wing sweep control screw jack
89 Wing pivot hinge fitting
90 Lateral longeron attachment joints
91 Wing pivot box carry-through
92 Wing sweep control jack hydraulic motor
93 Carry-through structure integral fuel tank
94 Upper longeron/carry-through joints
95 Starboard wing sweep control hydraulic motor
96 Wing sweep control screw jack
97 Starboard navigation light
98 Wing sweep pivot fixing
99 Wing root flexible seals
100 Aperture closing horn fairing
101 Flap/slat interconnecting drive shaft
102 Fuel pump
103 Fuel system piping
104 Starboard wing integral fuel tanks
105 Leading edge slat drive shaft
106 Slat guide rails
107 Slat screw jacks
108 Leading edge slat segments (7), open
109 Wing tip strobe light
110 Fuel system vent tank
111 Wing tip fairing
112 Static dischargers
113 Fuel jettison
114 Fixed portion of trailing edge
115 Starboard spoilers, open
116 Spoiler hydraulic jacks
117 Single-slotted Fowler-type flap, down position

118 Flap screw jacks
119 Flap guide rails
120 Wing root housing fairings
121 Dorsal spine fairing
122 Wheel bay dorsal fuel tank
123 Main undercarriage leg strut
124 Port main undercarriage, stowed position
125 Wheel bay avionics equipment racks
126 Fuselage lateral longeron
127 Wing root housing
128 Engine bleed air ducting
129 Ventral retractable air scoop
130 Fuel cooling heat exchanger
131 Heat exchanger spill air louvres
132 Rear rotary weapons dispenser
133 Control ducting
134 Tailplane longeron
135 Wing glove section tail fairing
136 Starboard wing fully swept position
137 Starboard engine exhaust nozzles
138 Longeron joint
139 Automatic stability and control system equipment (SCAS)

Left: The first B-1A seen from below in company with an F-111 chase aircraft, providing a clear comparison of SAC's two swing-wing bombers.

Right: This view gives an indication of the extra volume gained by the wing/body blending and the absence of radar trapping angles.

the wheel wells and in the structural compartments outboard of the gear. Behind the gear well is the aft weapons bay, again with integral fuel tanks, and from about halfway down the weapons bay double frames extend outboard to carry the engine nacelles. They reach as far as the nacelle centre beams. Finally, the aft fuselage section contains another fuel tank, another avionics bay and the dielectric tailcone.

Design of the aft fuselage section posed problems. Frames extending into the dorsal area give support and torsional stiffening to the tail assembly. The design of the horizontal tailplane was tailored around the stiffness originally specified, but it was later discovered that for the high-Q environment at low altitudes greater static strength would be needed. The obvious solution was to incorporate a dorsal spine made from steel alloy, which would be heavy but relatively cheap, but instead a five-section boron epoxy spine running from

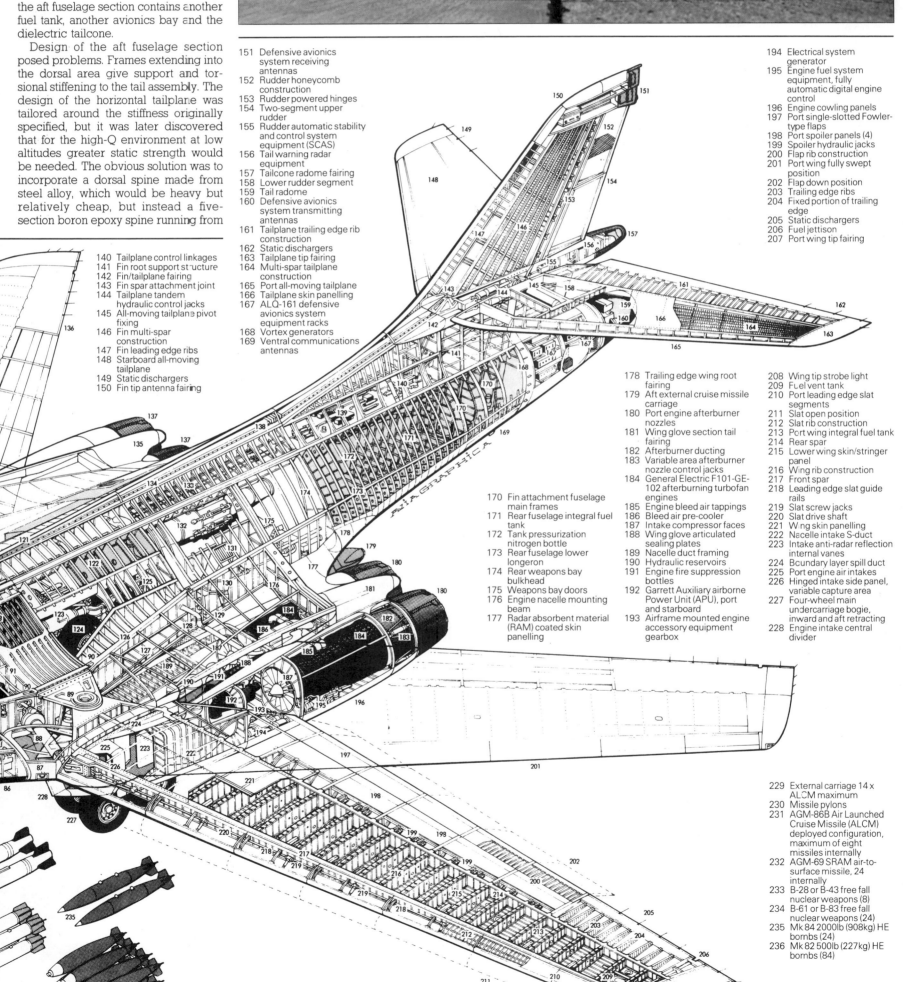

140 Tailplane control linkages
141 Fin root support structure
142 Fin/tailplane fairing
143 Fin spar attachment joint
144 Tailplane tandem hydraulic control jacks
145 All-moving tailplane pivot fixing
146 Fin multi-spar construction
147 Fin leading edge ribs
148 Starboard all-moving tailplane
149 Static dischargers
150 Fin tip antenna fairing
151 Defensive avionics system receiving antennas
152 Rudder honeycomb construction
153 Rudder powered hinges
154 Two-segment upper rudder
155 Rudder automatic stability and control system equipment (SCAS)
156 Tail warning radar equipment
157 Tailcone radome fairing
158 Lower rudder segment
159 Tail radome
160 Defensive avionics system transmitting antennas
161 Tailplane trailing edge rib construction
162 Static dischargers
163 Tailplane tip fairing
164 Multi-spar tailplane construction
165 Tailplane all-moving tailplane
166 Tailplane skin panelling
167 ALQ-161 defensive avionics system equipment racks
168 Vortex generators
169 Ventral communications antennas

170 Fin attachment fuselage main frames
171 Rear fuselage integral fuel tank
172 Tank pressurization nitrogen bottle
173 Rear fuselage lower longeron
174 Rear weapons bay bulkhead
175 Weapons bay doors
176 Engine nacelle mounting beam
177 Radar absorbent material (RAM) coated skin panelling
178 Trailing edge wing root fairing
179 Aft external cruise missile carriage
180 Port engine afterburner nozzles
181 Wing glove section tail fairing
182 Afterburner ducting
183 Variable area afterburner nozzle control jacks
184 General Electric F101-GE-102 afterburning turbofan engines
185 Engine bleed air tappings
186 Bleed air pre-cooler
187 Intake compressor faces
188 Wing glove articulated sealing plates
189 Nacelle duct framing
190 Hydraulic reservoirs
191 Engine fire suppression bottles
192 Garrett Auxiliary airborne Power Unit (APU), port and starboard
193 Airframe mounted engine accessory equipment gearbox

194 Electrical system generator
195 Engine fuel system equipment, fully automatic digital engine control
196 Engine cowling panels
197 Port single-slotted Fowler-type flaps
198 Port spoiler panels (4)
199 Spoiler hydraulic jacks
200 Flap rib construction
201 Port wing fully swept position
202 Flap down position
203 Trailing edge ribs
204 Fixed portion of trailing edge
205 Static dischargers
206 Fuel jettison
207 Port wing tip fairing
208 Wing tip strobe light
209 Fuel vent tank
210 Port leading edge slat segments
211 Slat open position
212 Slat rib construction
213 Port wing integral fuel tank
214 Rear spar
215 Lower wing skin/stringer panel
216 Wing rib construction
217 Front spar
218 Leading edge slat guide rails
219 Slat screw jacks
220 Slat drive shaft
221 Wing skin panelling
222 Nacelle intake S-duct
223 Intake anti-radar reflection internal vanes
224 Boundary layer spill duct
225 Port engine air intakes
226 Hinged intake side panel, variable capture area
227 Four-wheel main undercarriage bogie, inward and aft retracting
228 Engine intake central divider

229 External carriage 14 x ALCM maximum
230 Missile pylons
231 AGM-86B Air Launched Cruise Missile (ALCM) deployed configuration, maximum of eight missiles internally
232 AGM-69 SRAM air-to-surface missile, 24 internally
233 B-28 or B-43 free fall nuclear weapons (8)
234 B-61 or B-83 free fall nuclear weapons (24)
235 Mk 84 2000lb (908kg) HE bombs (24)
236 Mk 82 500lb (227kg) HE bombs (84)

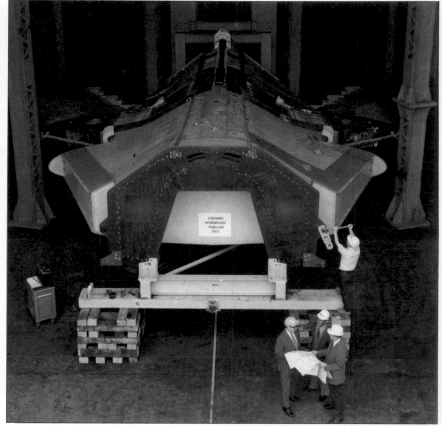

the WCT box to the base of the fin was selected. This offered at least as much static strength as steel and was much lighter, although more expensive. The proportion of composite material in the B-1A in terms of structural weight was very small; most of it was in this spine.

Fuselage changes between the B-1A and the B-1B were fairly major, although mainly beneath the surface. The fuel load carried by the B-1A at takeoff was restricted by the takeoff gross weight (TOGW) limit of 395,000lb (179,172kg), which meant it was dependent on IFR to carry out its mission, taking off with half-empty tanks and rendezvousing with a tanker before proceeding.

The TOGW of the B-1B was increased by a colossal 82,000lb (37,195kg) to 477,000lb (216,367kg) – which, as Rockwell's Scott L. White stressed at the 1985 Paris Air Show, was all additional fuel and weapons carriage capability: "The gross weight increase involved basically no empty weight increase to the aircraft. We didn't have 50,000lb (22,680kg) of structural weight to carry 32,000lb (14,515kg) extra weight of weapons and fuel. We were able to go through and reduce weight in several areas, and beef it up in others to carry this higher gross weight. We added a few thou here in wing skin thickness, and a few thou there in longerons, and did other things, like reworking the rear wing spar."

One main cause of the increase in TOGW was the carriage of external weapons; the other was the requirement that the aircraft be able to take off with a full fuel load. A stronger undercarriage and more powerful engines were the main factor in making this possible, and while Rockwell International's efforts to hold the empty weight constant represented an engineering *tour de force*, it is equally a testimony to the soundness of the original design.

Another major change between the B-1A and the B-1B resulted from alterations to the proposed weaponry. The basic B-1 has three weapons bays, each 15ft (4.57m) long, designed to accommodate the SRAM, and although the ALCM was originally intended to be similar in size later development work increased its length by nearly a third, so that it would no longer fit the B-1's weapons bay. The remedy was to make the front and intermediate weapons bays flexible by making the intervening bulkhead removable, providing a bay long enough

Above: The fin is fitted to the rear fuselage section of the first B-1B. The fuselage section at the join is nearly triangular, and has already been stuffed with the control and electrical connections.

to take the new ALCM, allowing growth space for new weapons and giving the option of carrying a small fuel tank at the front of the enlarged bay along with the ALCMs. This meant that structural loads in this area had to be carried through without the integral stiffening provided by the bulkhead.

The B-1A's weapons bay doors were metal, but the B-1B's are made of composites, which has both reduced radar reflectivity and improved acoustic characteristics, and on the B-1B an aerodynamic spoiler has been fitted to prevent the slipstream from entering the bays when the doors are open.

At the heart of the structure is the WCT box, a massive titanium structure likened by Rockwell to "the Brooklyn Bridge built like a Swiss watch". Its basic function is to carry the variable-geometry wings, but it also has to carry and support the main gear, in which function it must be able to cope with some 90 per cent of the maximum TOGW, and it also houses about 20,000lb (9,072kg) of fuel. Its overall length is something over 26ft (7.92m), it is 5ft (1.52m) from front to rear, and it is built in three large sections, mainly of diffusion bonded titanium.

Diffusion bonding

Diffusion bonding is a process developed by North American Rockwell for the XB-70 Valkyrie; in Scott L. White's words: "We get a large titanium plate, plus maybe about 40 smaller, individually machined pieces, and put them in a two-way box. The two-way box is a tool, and it accurately positions all those pieces. The tool is then evacuated, and subjected to high temperatures and pressures for between ten and twelve hours, it forms into one piece of material which needs little or no machining. It is just as though it has been cut from a single piece of metal. Then we weld two

Right: "The Brooklyn Bridge built like a Swiss watch", is how Rockwell describe the WCT box. Constructed mainly of diffusion bonded titanium, it supports the main undercarriage as well as the variable-sweep wings.

or three sections together to get a major section; the crossplates in the structure perform like an eggcrate."

The upper and lower cover then have to be fitted; the lower cover is duplicated, and the entire structure is designed to have a redundancy factor high enough that if one plate cracks the other can carry the entire load. Both upper and lower covers are bolted, using tapered bolts. These naturally need tapered holes. The taper is fairly marginal towards a point, and contributes considerably to structural strength. Tolerances on the whole unit are very tight – hence the Swiss watch analogy. As it is also a fuel tank, the WCT box is then sealed before undergoing a special heat process.

The pin on which the wing pivots is about 17in (430mm) in diameter and of the order of 600lb (272kg) in weight. Made of titanium, it is hollow, and is carried on a two-race spherical bearing.

The wing, a conventional two-spar aluminium box structure, with machined spars and ribs, also serves as a fuel tank and has machined aluminium single piece covers to both top and bottom. Segmented slats along the entire leading edge open only for takeoff, while a six-section single-slotted flap extends along most of the trailing edge, the two inner sections of which are locked closed when the wing sweep exceeds 20°. Roll control is by means of differentially moving tailplanes, assisted by spoilers on the upper wing surfaces, the outer sections of which also lock automatically at speeds exceeding Mach 1. The trail-

Above left: The front intermediate fuselage section is seen here mated to the WCT box and aft intermediate section, with wings already pinned in place. The cross section has changed appreciably at this point.

Above: The front fuselage section of the first B-1B is built in two halves, then stuffed with all the wiring and plumbing before the two halves are mated and the nose section, with its avionics bays, added in front.

Below: With only the aft fuselage section remaining to be mated, the varying concave sections to the area behind the cockpit are shown clearly by the differentially curving shapes of the open panels.

Above centre: The massive forged steel box support and spindle acts as a rear frame for the fuselage stub while joining both the fin and the stabilizers to the fuselage.

Above: The bottom section of the three-piece rudder, located below the horizontal tail, provides the SMCS control in the lateral plane, damping out unwanted yaw effects.

ing edge of the wing is notched where it joins the fuselage to preserve as much volume in the fuselage as possible when the wings are fully swept.

Wing fairing seals are always a problem on variable-geometry aircraft; even after wind-tunnel tests it is difficult to predict exactly how the full-scale article will behave, particularly in terms of drag. On the B-1A a hinged panel mounted behind the wing pivot line was fitted over the movable section of the wing as a fairing, backed by two fixed fairings blending the fuselage to the wing. The seal itself was a bulky and

expensive system of mechanical fingers designed to contour-articulate over the wing as it swept back, but this was draggy, heavy, complicated and costly, and when the B-1B was mooted, Rockwell examined all other alternatives. To the surprise of those who considered that the American aerospace industry led the world in every field, the best system was found to be that adopted for Europe's Panavia Tornado of sliding 'feathers' supported by an inflatable bag, and this was duly incorporated into the design of the B-1B. The inflatable bags, made by the Chesterfield, England, firm

Left: Fully assembled, the first B-1B is seen undergoing a thorough systems checkout at Palmdale prior to rollout. The black areas on and around the SMCS vanes are probably radar absorbent material (RAM).

of Woodville Polymers, are 20ft (6.10m) long, and each has 21 pressure relief valves, also British-produced by Normalair-Garrett of Yeovil.

It was originally planned to have an empennage of composite construction, but that on the B-1A was primarily of aluminium. The fin consisted of a single box component, attached to the aft fuselage with a double shear attachment and bolted to the horizontal stabilizer spindle. The rudder was in three sections, two above the line of the horizontal stabilizer and one below, the last being linked to the low-altitude ride control, and the design and sizing of the horizontal tail surfaces was largely determined by flutter characteristics.

The horizontal stabilizers were also of aluminium box construction, with GRP leading and trailing edges and tips. The structure was fitted directly onto the steel spindle and the two surfaces rotated independently of each other to give both pitch and roll control, with deflections of 10° up and 25° down for pitch control and plus or minus 20° for roll. Flight testing showed that under extreme aerodynamic loads the stabilizers had insufficient authority in both pitch and roll; this was overcome by altering the hinge point to limit the moment on successive aircraft.

Composite construction, scheduled to be used for the stabilizers on the fifth and succeeding B-1As, is a feature of the B-1B, for which advanced composite technology has been used to build both horizontal and vertical tail surfaces; the structures of both are now of high strength titanium sine wave beams – hailed as a breakthrough in advanced welding processes and unique in the aerospace industry.

Developed by Rockwell in conjunction with Martin Marietta, the subcontractor for the tail surfaces, the process achieves maximum strength and integrity with minimum weight penalty; the beams are very similar to standard structural I-beams, but the central section is very precisely corrugated to match sine wave dimensions, and narrow caps of titanium sheet are welded to the edge of the corrugation; the sine wave is tracked from the outside of the cap by the welding torch, using heat sensors.

At the heart of the tailplane assembly is a massive box support and spindle, forged from HP9-4-20 steel alloy and weighing about 4,950lb (2,245kg). This huge spindle is a major structural component which not only serves as a rear frame for the fuselage stub beneath the fin, but also joins both the fin and the stabilizers to the fuselage while supporting the bottom of the three rudders.

One of the most innovative, if not the most obvious features of the B-1 is the Structural Mode Control System (SMCS), which in its early days was known as the Low Altitude Ride Control (LARC). Penetration of defended areas at high subsonic speeds and very low altitudes is a good way to evade detection and interception, but the turbulence encountered near ground level gives rise to bumps. These can be very severe; for example, a B-52 travelling at a fairly sedate 325kt (602km/h) and 1,000ft (305m) can experience gust loads of +4g and −2g in the cockpit, even in moderately turbulent conditions, as a result of aeroelastic fuselage whipping.

A large aircraft is more prone to this flexing effect than a small one, and the

faster it flies the worse it gets. Under these conditions the aircraft is difficult to control, the instruments are difficult to read and making the correct switch selections becomes a matter of great care, and a prolonged period of low-level flight lowers crew efficiency significantly. The solution to the problem was the SMCS.

After the Valkyrie bomber programme had been cancelled the two flying examples had undertaken a research programme, mainly into high-altitude very high-speed flight, but also into the effects of turbulence on large high-speed aircraft. Exciter vanes had been installed on an XB-70 as part of the latter programme, providing the basis for SMCS. The basic idea is that small canard surfaces on the nose of a long aircraft can damp out the bumps by providing forces that will oppose flexing, and in the early days of the B-1 project it was calculated that the system could reduce the vertical acceleration loadings to barely one-third of their undamped level. Lateral loading would need to be taken care of by means of yaw dampers. The only alternative would be to increase the rigidity of the aircraft and thus reduce the bouncing effect at the extremities, but Rockwell calculations showed that this approach would have incurred a penalty of 5-10,000lb (2,268-4,536kg) in weight. By contrast, the SMCS weighed in at just under 500lb (227kg)

SMCS operation

SMCS is an automatically controlled system which uses two small vanes, mounted either side of the nose at a pronounced anhedral angle, and the bottom section of the three piece rudder. When switched on the system responds to accelerometer signals which detect turbulence and react very rapidly, damping out lateral motion through the rudder section, while the vertical motion is corrected primarily by the nose vanes, which can travel through an arc of plus or minus 20° at speeds of up to 200°/sec. The system is reported to be working better than anticipated; there was originally some mistrust on the part of certain pilots, but experience quickly converted them. On the B-1A, the nose vanes were of aluminium, but on the B-1B they are primarily of graphite epoxy bonded to an aluminium honeycomb, with titanium leading and trailing edges and mounted on a steel trunnion superstructure.

The engines are mounted in pods under the wing gloves. The intakes were the subject of a complete redesign for the B-1B, as described in the following chapter.

Another area of major redesign was the cockpit, although as we have seen, this was part of the B-1A development programme. The original scheme had been for a crew escape module with close to zero/zero adverse attitude capability, the design of which had been based on that of the General Dynamics F-111. This had been chosen because it offered the best survival prospects for the crew in the event of a stratospheric bale-out at Mach 2, while performing well at high subsonic speeds and low altitudes, and improving crew efficiency by permitting a shirt-sleeve operating environment. It was also water-tight, and would remain afloat in the sea, and in the event of an ejection over inhospitable terrain it would provide shelter for the crew while they awaited rescue. Finally, initial studies predicted a weight saving with its use.

The crew escape module was fitted to the first three aircraft only. Separation is initiated by pulling either the pilot's or the co-pilot's ejection handles, or both rear seat ejecting handles, whereupon

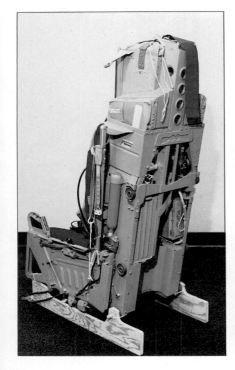

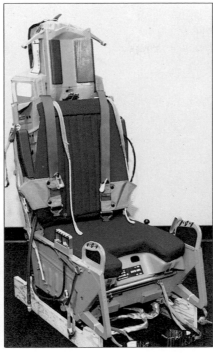

Above: Three-quarter rear view of the ACES ejection seat fitted to all production aircraft. It has zero/zero capability for low-level emergency ejections.

Above: The ACES ejection seat from the front, showing the harness and the leg restraints and the padded headrest designed to prevent whiplash injuries to the occupant's neck.

an explosive system shears the module from the aircraft, a drogue parachute is deployed, and a pair of fins situated on top of the fuselage extend to stabilize it during the deceleration period. During this time a rocket motor flies the module automatically to a safe altitude and attitude, and when sufficient speed has been lost three recovery parachutes are released; a five-bladder landing impact attenuator system inflates before ground contact.

Entry to the module was through a belly hatch by means of an extending ladder, and an emergency exit hatch was also incorporated. The crew section could be pressurized for an equivalent altitude of 8,000ft (2,438m), while an unpressurized section housed the escape chutes and rocket motor system. The module was exhaustively tested, with 48 major parachute tests, ten aerial drops of the module, 17 stabilization component sled tests, and five crew escape module sled tests, but it was eventually rejected due to instability in certain flight regimes, although it was also found to be very expensive to maintain, and removal for checking was a complex and time-consuming operation. A temporary bulkhead had to be inserted in the junction frames to maintain the structural integrity of the aircraft while it was removed, and an incredible number of systems had to be discon-

Above: The crew escape module used on the first three B-1As is seen here carried inverted beneath the wing of a B-52 as part of intensive proof of concept trials.

Above: The crew escape module about to impact during trials. The fins can be seen deployed at the rear, and the impact attenuation bags are fully inflated for landing.

Below: The crew board what appears to be the fourth B-1A. The first man to arrive hits a switch on the nose gear which starts the APUs, providing power to the systems.

Above: The construction of the heavy and complicated nose gear is clearly depicted, with the figure alongside giving scale. The good downward visibility over the nose is apparent from this angle.

Right: In-flight view over the nose while traversing the Grand Canyon at low level. The photograph appears to have been taken from the co-pilot's seat, with the result that the forward view is slightly degraded.

nected, then reconnected on completion. From the fourth prototype onward the module was deleted and ACES II ejection seats substituted.

The crew of the B-1 normally consists of the pilot, co-pilot, and two avionics systems operators, one for the defensive and one for the offensive systems. Provision also has to be made for two instructors, and in the early days of the project the possibility of carrying two extra crewmen was considered, in order to fly missions of up to 36 hours. The cockpit of the B-1B is fairly roomy, allows the crew to get up and stretch, and incorporates a hot cup and a chemical convenience, while the avionics operators also have a window in the B-1B, presumably for psychological reasons. The instructors position leaves a little to be desired – the four regular crew positions all have ejection seats, but the instructors are left to depart manually through the belly hatch – but overall the B-1 is a remarkably comfortable aeroplane; the longest flight to date, from Edwards to Farnborough in 1982, lasted 11 hours 25 minutes, and the crew reported no undue fatigue at the end of the trip.

Forward visibility is excellent: the nose slopes steeply away to give good vision for landing, and the windshields are large, with overhead transparencies for a vertical view which is necessary during in-flight refuelling. The windshields themselves consist of an outer glass layer, which provides an abrasion and heat resistant surface, combined with an electrical demisting and deicing system, and an inner 12mm ply lightweight, high impact-resistant polycarbonate plastic layer which incorporates a 4mm thick spall shield on the inside face; the entire structure is bonded with a silicone interlayer material resistant to temperature changes. The windshield is designed to withstand a birdstrike of 4lb (1.81kg) at a speed of 600kt (1,112km/h).

The cockpit is also the nerve centre of the flight control system. In the early design stage, fly-by-wire was in its infancy and its use was considered to be a

technical risk, so it was decided to go for a complete electro-hydraulic control system, using rods, cables, pulleys and bell-crank levers, with linear gearing to the flight controls. It was quadruplex, and consisted of four simultaneously operating but independent hydraulic systems functioning at 4,000psi, systems 1 and 2 running off the two left-hand engines while 3 and 4 were powered by the right-hand engines. The mission can be completed with a single system failure, while a double failure permits a safe landing.

A 4,000psi system represented the state of the art at that time; most other aircraft used 3,000psi systems, though a notable exception was Tornado, which made its maiden flight some three months earlier. This entirely mechanical system involved penalties in space and weight, but was felt to be justified by the reliability of a tried and trusted system,

Right: The main gear is designed to be able to cope with 90 per cent of the B-1B's takeoff gross weight of more than 220 tonnes on landing, though seen from this angle, it looks decidedly flimsy for the task.

while the higher pressure produced weight savings.

The Automatic Flight Control System (AFCS) provided roll attitude, flight path, airspeed, auto-throttle and Mach holds. A systems routing tunnel is provided in the upper fuselage structure between the longerons, while the wing sweep actuators and flap and slot drive mechanisms are located in the forward intermediate fuselage, in the wing blended section. The Sundstrand wing sweep actuation system was (and probably still is) the largest aircraft actuation system in the world. Another first is the hinge-line geared rotary actuation system for the rudder, also by Sundstrand, which had never before been used in a production aircraft.

The B-1B contained certain changes to the flight control system. Non-linear gearing was introduced to improve handling, particularly for the precision flying involved in in-flight refuelling, and fly-by-wire was introduced alongside the mechanical controls, the pilot's control system being FBW while the co-pilot's system is mechanical. This produces a considerable saving in weight, although it is safeguarded by a rever-

Above: The cockpit transparencies are designed to give good front quarter vision, while those overhead are used mainly in air refuelling. It can be seen that a marginal view behind the beam is possible.

sionary link in which if one system fails, the two sets of controls can be tied together. This provides systems redundancy. The wing spoilers were modified to eradicate a tendency to float up.

The undercarriage consists of a rather long main gear with two four-wheel bogies which retracts into the centre fuselage section, with a twin-wheel nose gear retracting forward into a well beneath the crew compartment. The fuselage ground clearance is about 9ft (2.74m), while the engine nacelle clearance is about half this distance, and retraction or extension is completed in 12 seconds by means of electronically controlled actuators.

The gear is designed to cope with nearly 90 per cent of the TOGW when landing and is accordingly substantial, the main landing gear cylinders being forged from 300M steel and weighing roughly 3,000lb (1,361kg) each while the nose gear, which is not subject to the same stresses, has a main cylinder forged from 7175 aluminium alloy and weighs in at 1,000lb (454kg). No reverse thrust or braking parachute is fitted, but five-rotor carbon type brakes are supplied by Goodyear, who also make the tyres. Ground steering is provided by the nose wheel, which can turn through 76° right or left or, for manoeuvring by support vehicles in confined spaces, can be released to give full 360° rotation.

The B-1 was designed to be survivable, not only in the accepted sense of surviving battle damage and successfully penetrating hostile defence zones, but also in the event of a surprise nuclear attack. While nothing can ensure survival of an aircraft in the event of a near miss, there is much that can be done to maximize the chances of survival and serviceability to carry out the mission.

The hazards from a nuclear explosion are blast, heat, overpressure and radiation. A certain amount can be done to minimize the effects of the first three by strengthening the structure, although too much strength is counter-productive as the weight increase rapidly becomes prohibitive, but this is a sensitive area,

Left: Nose gear retraction tests at Rockwell's Palmdale facility. The plethora of hydraulic lines and wires within the gear bay are seen as the gear retracts forwards.

and no specific details of blast and overpressure hardening have been released. The original B-1As were painted white as a protection against flash, but with the increasing accent on low level penetration this ceased to be acceptable; white would make the defending interceptors' task easier by day or in moonlight by highlighting the aircraft against the terrain below.

The compromise mooted for the B-1B was to use light and dark grey camouflage, which would break up the outline of the aircraft in low level flight, with the light grey used to cover the heat-sensitive zones such as the avionics compartments and the flight deck. This scheme was dropped, and production B-1Bs are sprayed in the European One scheme of Dark Olive Green, Dark Green and Dark Grey, although the constantly changing angle of the light on the sweeping curves, and the deliberate use of paints of varying reflective qualities, makes this difficult to discern clearly. The approach has been to concentrate on a feature that will actively assist the completion of the mission rather than one that will aid survival in what must be marginal circumstances at the outset.

The main enemy in the event of a surprise nuclear attack is radiation in the form of Electromagnetic Pulse (EMP), which is capable of disrupting or completely destroying electronic circuits. Even such large and coarse things as street lights can be affected, and an aircraft like the B-1, packed with electronic gadgetry, is very vulnerable, and there would be little point in surviving the blast, heat, and overpressure of a nuclear explosion only to find that the vital avionic systems had all been taken out. A lot of research has gone into solving this problem, much of it by the avionic system contractors, but certain items have been incorporated into the structure and can be described here, although others cannot be commented on as yet.

Basically, guarding against EMP involves shielding wiring with overbraided cable, or, in areas such as the avonics compartments, where the density of wiring would make this impractical, by shielding the entire compartment with a contrivance similar to a Faraday cage. Avionics bays and doors are also

Below: The first step in inserting a wing pivot pin is to shrink the pin by immersion in liquid nitrogen. This is done at the assembly point by engineers specially suited and visored against spillage.

Bottom: Positioning the pivot pin takes about five minutes, but the assembly is expected to remain in place for 30 years, making precision of manufacture and positioning of components to exact clearances vital.

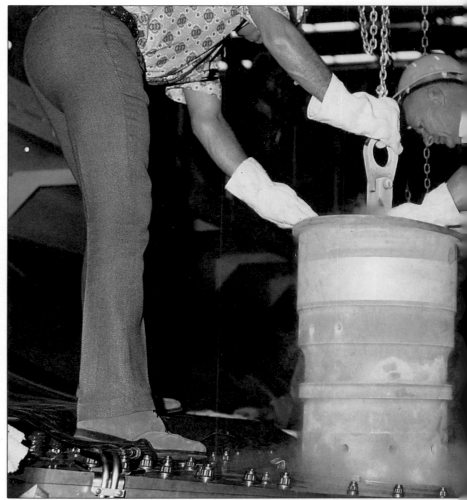
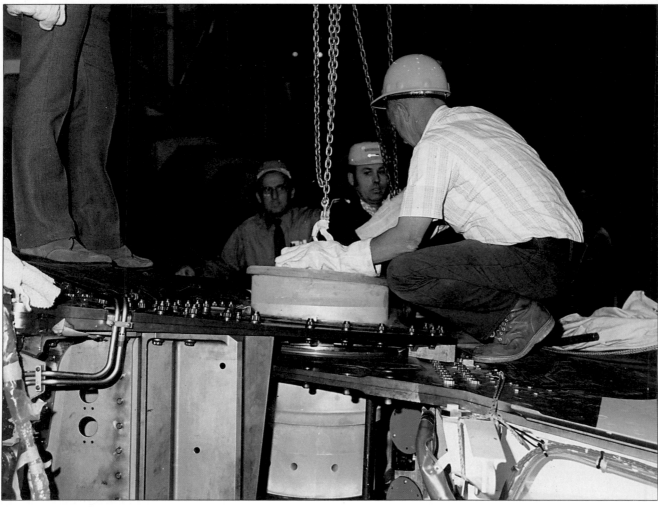

shielded by creating paths of low electrical resistance around them, again using braided cables. By these means, it is hoped, the EMP will be diverted from sensitive systems.

Central to the mission of the B-1 is its ability to penetrate hostile defences unseen and undetected, and since air defence systems are heavily reliant on radar, a lot of effort has gone into reducing the bomber's RCS. As we saw earlier, the small RCS of the B-1A was largely a spin-off from the evolving design: in the beginning, ECM was expected to be the principal form of protection. Quite early in the programme it was discovered that the B-1 would have a very small RCS compared

with that of the B-52 – authoritatively quoted by certain European magazines as either 1/35 or 1/25 the latter's.

Of course, the study of radar signatures was at that time in its infancy; there was probably no deliberate intent to mislead anyone. So what is the truth? The RCS of the B-1A is widely stated to have been 1/10 of that of the B-52, while the RCS of the B-1B is equally widely stated to be 1/10 of that of the B-1A. The B-52 is reckoned to have an RCS of $100m^2$, which would make that of the B-1B just $1m^2$. For comparison, a normal fighter sized target is reckoned to be about $5m^2$, while the small MiG-21 is supposed to have an RCS of $2m^2$ from the head-on (ie, smallest) aspect. In fact, the RCS of the B-1B is highly classified information, despite the fact that the above figures are widely reported even in official USAF releases; but we can be certain that the B-1A was a vast improvement over the B-52, and that the B-1B shows a further reduction in RCS.

The improvement shown by the B-1A was primarily a result of its less reflective shape, while the B-1B was the subject of an extensive programme to reduce radar reflectivity in three areas: avionics, structure and radar absorbent material (RAM). As far as avionics were concerned, the main change was to the radar antenna, as described in the Avionics chapter. Structurally, the

Left: The cooled pin is lowered into position in an area prewarmed by heating blankets to increase the tolerance; the fitters have to wear special gloves. The minute precision of the WCT box can be seen.

Below left: The engineers in their special suits make final adjustments from underneath, fitting what seems to be a ring collar. The double titanium wing connector plate is clearly visible from this angle.

Below: The second B-1A prototype, the structural test vehicle, is seen here undergoing airframe proof and calibration evaluation in Lockheed-California Company's structural test rig at Palmdale.

engine inlets were completely redesigned to reduce radar signature, a change dealt with in the Propulsion chapter; more significantly, the front and rear bulkheads were canted downward so that radar pulses meet them at an oblique angle and are more likely to be scattered than reflected straight back. Both these changes, very worthwhile in themselves, were made even more effective by the extensive use of RAM.

The search for a radar absorbent material was started by the German Navy during World War II. The Kriegsmarine wanted to make its U-boats invisible to British airborne radar, something beyond the state of the art for a number of years, but in fairly recent times a radar absorbent coating has been developed which can capture the tiny electronic impulses emitted by radar and convert them into heat instead of reflecting them back. It was not perfect, but it reduced the radar echo considerably.

RAM applications

The RAM used on the B-1A and B-1B is, once again, a sensitive subject, and no specific details are forthcoming, but it is widely known that RAM materials are sensitive to wavelength, and that what works on one wavelength will not work on another. The problem with the B-1 was simplified by its flying at low level, where the only wavelengths likely to be used against it were those in the 3cm I/J band. Although it can only be speculation, it seems likely that the RAM used on the B-1B is optimized for this wavelength, where it will be most effective.

Having developed the material, the designers had to decide where to locate it for the best effect. The engine intakes were one obvious choice, and RAM was used extensively in this area even on the B-1A. For the rest, the fore and aft canted bulkheads were shrouded with the substance, because they were behind cones made of dielectric material transparent to radar signals, and it is also applied around the glove vanes, on the front of the wing fairing and wing root fairings, around the spoilers and flaps and on the horizontal stabilizers – anywhere, in fact, that there is an angle that

could trap and reflect back radar energy.

In fact, with an aeroplane so packed with avionics, it has been an exercise of considerable ingenuity to allow the sensors, both active and passive, to look out, detect and positively identify threat radars, while actively deflecting or absorbing their emissions in other areas. Another problem has been the flight deck transparencies: a threat radar could look right through these, and receive an echo from the interior, so an electrically conducting coating was developed to channel the impulses away. All in all, defeating enemy radars by passive means such as clever design and special materials has been a major task, brilliantly executed.

The construction of the B-1B has been a major operation, and a list of the companies involved reads like a directory of the American aerospace industry. Apart from the four associate contractors, there are 50 major subcontractors and over 3,000 suppliers. At the peak of the programme, Rockwell International estimate that no fewer than 50,000 people will be working on the project, including 22,000 directly employed by Rockwell in plants at Palmdale, El Segundo, Colombus and Tulsa. Early in 1986 production was ahead of schedule (the first B-1B was delivered some months ahead of time), and exactly on budget.

Some of the statistics are mind-boggling. The B-1B has required some 18,000 engineering drawings, 61,000 manufacturing orders have been placed, and 25 five-axis milling machines, which can cut and grind metals to an almost infinite variety of shapes, have been acquired. No fewer than 460,500 individual items are required as spares for each aircraft, and 4,800 items of support equipment, of which nearly three-quarters are peculiar to the B-1B.

Structural testing, which began in 1970, was designed to develop processing and fabrication methods and to check strength limitations of structural elements and assembled components. An exhaustive series of tests included more than 2,000 on materials, 2,600 on fracture mechanics and 2,400 on fastener

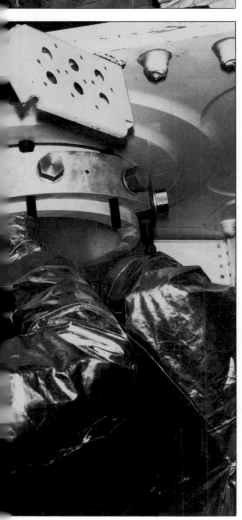

Above: A busy scene at Palmdale, with assembly work on the first B-1B finally approaching completion. An interesting detail evident here is the nacelle fairing between the starboard engine effluxes.

Left: The size and shape of the B-1 mean that a large number of work stands have to be employed. The wing/body blending necessitates a special stand on the aft fuselage.

tion or a junction occurs a mockup of the fitting needed is made and check-fitted into the SDT. Once its correctness is established, the mockup piece is fed into a numerically controlled machine which records the exact specifications, and these are in turn fed into a bending machine, which produces the actual hardware to very tight tolerances.

Close tolerances, complexity and planning are the three main factors in the production process. Planning includes organizing the material flow, so that everything is in its appointed place at the proper time, and getting the optimum major sections broken down to give maximum production rates.

Questioned on the production process, Scott L. White explained: "It's all very similar to the B-1A except for the forward fuselage and the nacelles. These are the two critical paths, the forward fuselage because the preponderance of wiring is in it, and the nacelles because they had to be completely redesigned, and we had to start from scratch. What we were originally going to do on the forward fuselage was to build it in what we call the 'cigar', but

systems; altogether, 682 specimens were used to establish the basic design concepts, check out the exact configurations and verify the predicted results.

The next stage comprised Design Verification Tests (DVTs), in which nine full-scale sections, all structurally critical, were put through extensive fatigue and static tests. The WCT box was the most important of these: static tests were carried out for 12 simulated flight conditions, four of them with the gear down, with the wing sweep varied from 15° to 67½°. The WCT box was also tested to

100 per cent of its design limit loading on a dozen occasions, and once taken to 150 per cent of the design loading without failure.

Materials selection also came under close scrutiny. The B-1 was the first major programme to have a fracture mechanics requirement, and much emphasis was placed on developing techniques to measure and control the fracture resistance of aluminium, steel, and titanium. One of the main findings was that much closer quality control had to be exercised.

Located at Rockwell's El Segundo plant, the System Development Tool (SDT) is virtually a mockup of the full size aircraft. Originally built in sections for the B-1A programme, it was later modified to represent the B-1B and assembled into a complete structure. Its function is to allow planning and manufacture of the wires, cables, and tubing that make up the intestines of the aircraft.

For example, the route of a particular system is planned to fit in with the other systems that must also pass through the same area, and where a change in direc-

B-1B structural components

First stage in the mating of primary structural assemblies is the attachment of forward intermediate and aft intermediate fuselage sections to the wing carry-through box. The vertical stabilizer is attached to the aft fuselage section before it and the **forward fuselage are joined to the intermediate fuselage structures; then comes installation of the nacelles, undercarriage, wings and horizontal stabilizers. Engines and landing gear and weapons bay doors are added during final installation.**

then we had all the people in the world doing the wiring inside it and getting in each other's way.

"What we have done now is to split this section in half, and the majority of the wiring, amounting to about 35,000 wire segments, is done in a separate building. It really cuts down on time and big problems. On the assembly line there is a tram, and each half section runs down to the final assembly position. The assembly line has five mate stations where the entire fuselage is put together. We have generated a lot of capability and quality in this process, and we also utilize a lot of automatic fastenings. The system is that the automatic fastening machine drills the hole and serves the fastener. If it happens to be in a fuel containing area, it also automatically puts the sealer in. All this improves the quality and repeatability from aircraft to aircraft.

Wing mating procedure

"When the fuselage is assembled, the landing gear is attached, then it is rolled forward on the gear to the wing mating stations. No levelling equipment is needed to assemble the wings because only at one point do they attach. The wings are on tools [jigs] and the tools are on airglides. The fuselage is pulled in between the wings, and then the wing is pushed into position by three men. To fix the wing pivot pin, heating blankets are placed on the wing carriage fittings to warm and expand them, while the pin is put into liquid nitrogen to shrink it. The pin, which is hollow, is then lifted out by crane and dropped into position; it takes about five minutes. As long as we do it

Right: The B-1B project embraces more than 5,000 subcontractors and suppliers: here the first aft intermediate fuselage arrives by Super Guppy at Palmdale from Vought Aero products in Dallas.

within fifteen minutes there is no problem. The men have to wear special gloves. Then the final touches are applied, and the job is done."

However meticulous the planning, things still go wrong. Murphy's First Law provides that if a thing can be put on upside down, sooner or later it will be, and it duly happened with the first production B-1B, although it should be pointed out that Rockwell were not at fault. On the upper fitting that joins the WCT box to the wing there is a bearing which is not quite concentric, and the supplier is supposed to stamp it "this side up". Unfortunately, the supplier stamped the wrong side; the bearings were put in upside down and the wing pins were inserted, then Rockwell performed the final measurements to check that the clearances were correct, whereupon the error was discovered. The wing would function as it was, but would be subject to fatigue and wear, and would not meet the 30-year life requirement.

Now, this particular aircraft was scheduled to join the test programme: it was not going to be subject to the stresses of operational aircraft, and the temptation must have existed to let it pass, then take remedial action at a later date. Against this, the B-1B programme was a fishbowl, subject to intense public scrutiny, not only for performance and cost, but also quality. Had the press got

hold of the story, they would have had a field day, and faith in the programme would have been seriously undermined.

The discovery was made at about midday on a Thursday. Within hours, the decision had been made to pull both pins. Somewhere along the line this would have to be done anyway; the Air Force would need to know the correct procedures and the method would have to be physically verified when the manual was prepared. So the procedures were scheduled, with video cameras installed to record events, and

the engineers went to work.

The method was the reverse of the installation procedure: the hollow pins were filled with liquid nitrogen to shrink them, the crane was positioned, and one pin came straight out; the other stuck slightly but virtually no difficulty was encountered. By the morning of the following Monday, the pins had been pulled and the bearings checked and replaced correctly. In Scott White's words: "We went back to the supplier and made sure that it could never happen again."

Powerplant

The AMSA specification, with its emphasis on low-level penetration, called for an engine that was both economical and flexible: the answer was the General Electric F101 turbofan. During the long gestation of the B-1B, however, the priorities changed, so that supersonic speed lost much of its initial importance and the high-speed, low-level flight regime became paramount, allied to durability and reliability. In producing the F101-102 derivative of the original F101-100, General Electric also had to meet a requirement for neutral installation, enabling any engine to be installed in either side of either nacelle.

The choice of qualities for the engine to power the B-1 naturally involved trade-offs between certain desirable features. The demands of the mission were: unre-fuelled intercontinental range; sustained high subsonic speeds in the turbulent air found at low levels; and high initial thrust to get it out of a short airfield. The first three put a premium on fuel economy, which in turn dictated the use of a turbofan with a relatively high bypass ratio for a military aircraft, and the new engine was derived from a General Electric test programme designated GE9 Phase II, a demonstrator of which had been produced in 1965.

Development started in that year at the same time as the AMSA studies, and culminated in the award on June 5, 1970, of a USAF contract for the development of 40 YF101-GE-100 engines, a quantity reduced to 27 when the number of proto-type B-1s was cut back. The design goals can be summarized by a simple comparison with two J79s: a single YF101 was intended to do the same amount of work

Left: An F101-GE-100 undergoing a full throttle run in a test rig at night. Comparison with pictures of fighter engines in similar tests reveals a bigger and more visible exhaust plume.

Above: Underside view of the right engine nacelle of the third B-1A, showing the excellent access to the engines afforded by removing a two-part cowl. The inner engine nozzle is contracted, the outer dilated.

while occupying less than 30 per cent of the volume, with an improvement on the specific fuel consumption (sfc) at cruising speed of about 25 per cent and with no visible smoke emission.

The turbofan engine is basically a standard jet engine with an oversized fan in the front acting as a low pressure compressor. The throughput of air from the intake is therefore much larger than that in a pure jet engine, and this produces a high-mass exhaust of lower velocity. Much of the air from the intakes is led around the engine core and does not pass through the engine proper. This is termed the bypass, and the bypass ratio refers to the amount of air which passes the engine in relation to the amount that actually goes through it.

Below: Cutaway of the original B-1 engine, the F101-GE-100. The length of the power-producing core, from the compressor to the augmentor rings, can be seen to be barely half of the total engine length.

General Electric F101-GE-100 turbofan

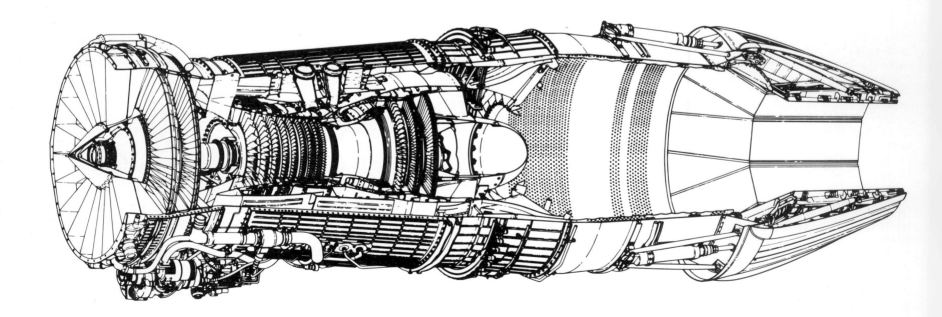

The fan is driven by a spool from the turbine, which is in turn driven by the compressed and heated air from the combustion chambers. Modern airliners typically use a high bypass ratio engine which is very efficient at subsonic speeds, producing a lot of thrust for a relatively small amount of fuel. The bypass air also serves a cooling function, enabling higher turbine temperatures to be used than would otherwise be the case, which further increases efficiency. Much of the inherent efficiency of the turbofan is lost at supersonic speeds and high altitudes, and for a high-performance aircraft the bypass ratio must be carefully sized to give the best possible combination of performance throughout the flight envelope.

The F101 is a twin spool turbofan engine with an original bypass ratio of 2.2:1, later reduced to 2:1, which means that twice as much air goes through the bypass as through the core. This figure is relatively high for a fast jet engine, as we can see by comparing it with the slightly earlier TF30 that powers the F-14 and the F100 powerplant of the F-15 and F-16, whose bypass ratios are 0.9 and 0.7 respectively.

The F101 features two fan compressor stages and nine high-pressure (HP) compressor stages driven by two low-pressure (LP) and one HP turbine stages. The average pressure rise per compressor stage is 1.35:1, far exceeding the 1.20 and 1.25:1 of the TF30 and F100, for a total pressure ratio of 27:1, some 50 per cent higher than that of the fighter engines. Thrust in both military power and full augmentation of 17,000lb (75.6kN) and 30,000lb (133.4kN) respectively also far exceeded the power of the TF30 and the F100. But they were designed to meet an altogether different mission requirement; the driving factor for the B-1 engines was power with economy to meet the demanding operational radius tempered with speed requirements.

In fact, the F101 was later optimized to meet fighter needs, first as the F101DFE (Derivative Fighter Engine) and subse-

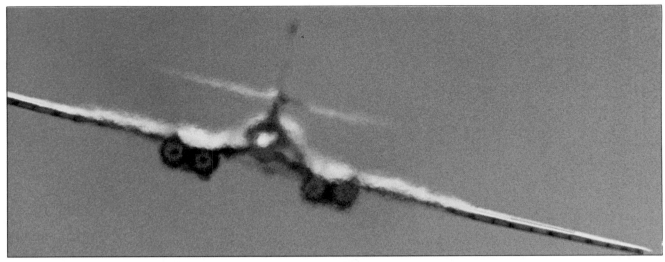

Top: This rear view of the second B-1A using full augmentation shows the low visibility of the engines when seen from astern in daylight, while the exhaust plume is for all practical purposes smoke-free.

Above: Same aircraft, same day, slightly different angle showing the nozzles dilated. The spacing between engines in each nacelle is an insurance against damage to one affecting the other.

Below: Four YF101 flight test engines at Rockwell's Palmdale facility, ready to be installed in a B-1A. A total of 46 YF101s were built, of which half had been delivered to Rockwell by 1977, when B-1A production was cancelled.

Top left: The mission profile of the B-1 calls for quick reaction and good short field capability, demonstrated here by the second B-1A prototype.

Left upper centre: The same aircraft demonstrates a two-engined takeoff. No significant asymmetric handling problems have been found.

Left lower centre: The B-1A demonstrates single-engined flight, the pilot using a large bootful of left rudder to stay straight.

Left: Finally, an unaugmented (non-afterburning) takeoff is demonstrated. Although this requires a reduction in takeoff gross weight and a long runway, it is quite within the B-1's capabilities.

quently the F110, which has been selected to power later versions of all three fighters. The core of the DFE is virtually identical to that of the F101, but the bypass ratio has been lowered to 0.85 an extra fan stage has been added and the overall pressure ratio has been increased to 30:1, to produce slightly more thrust at military power, and about 10 per cent less at full augmentation. On the other hand, the weight and frontal area have been reduced, the specific thrust shows a considerable improvement and throttle response is more rapid. This is not to imply that either engine is better than the other; each is best for the task for which it was designed.

June 1971 saw the Initial Design Review (IDR), which was carried out by the USAF, and a full-scale engine mock-

viding enough power for all the aircraft systems.

The F101 has been claimed to be America's most tested engine. The original F101 development programme had contained many new concepts, such as multiple milestones and non-concurrent development and production etc, and the first flight of the B-1A, on December 23, 1974, was to be followed by two very important milestones: the completion of the Product Verification Programme (PVP) by mid-1976; and the key item for the entire B-1 project, DSARC III, the production decision, which was scheduled for November 1976. Meanwhile, the USAF had been considering alternative test programmes, and between 1970 and 1974, analysis had been conducted in parallel with the development of the F101, though without impinging on it.

Most of the problems in previous engine programmes had stemmed from the lack of a good aeromechanical data base over the entire flight envelope, and from differences between operational usage and endurance testing during the development phase. In other words, the theoretical data on which previous test programmes had been based bore little relationship to what actually happened when the operational units got their hands on the hardware, and as aircraft became more capable, they were being used much harder than had been foreseen, whereas during the development programme, test pilots flew strictly regulated flight profiles which were related to ground test data. Consequently, there was a tendency for weaknesses to show up only when the aircraft reached the squadrons, a little late in the day for remedial action to be taken. Also, there had been an emphasis on either meeting

performance and/or weight limits in full; this had often led to a tradeoff with reliability, through squeezing the last ounce out of the new engine.

After extensive reviews of past programmes, the Air Force Aeronautical Systems Division devised a method of improving the development process. The emphasis was on achieving the initial operational Time Between Overhauls (TBO), and the development engines (YF) were to be used to attain a balance between performance, weight, cost, reliability and durability rather than attaining one absolute figure at the expense of any other. Furthermore, it was suggested that development should be aimed more at the production engines at the expense of the pre-production examples, while the post-Product Verification (PV) phase prior to the production phase should be used to examine logistics and maintenance aspects. This was called the New Development Concept.

In 1974 the Air Force System Program Office decided to adapt the New Development concept to the F101 programme, which was already well advanced, and a comprehensive review of the entire programme followed. At that time, the programme for the F101 was the most detailed ever, containing all the elements of the past engine programmes with extra design and testing requirements in the areas of airframe compatibility, low cycle fatigue, and structural integrity. Certain military specifications had been identified as unnecessary, where past results had proved irrelevant, or the items were covered by component testing, items eliminated including the ingestion of sand, and salt water.

Examination of the endurance testing

schedule for the F101 revealed some anomalies. The requirement was based on a modified milspec, but in many areas it failed to cover the B-1A's operational profile, with the maximum thrust limits for takeoff and climb too low by a substantial margin, while supersonic cruising had been overestimated by almost a factor of three. Worst of all, there was no provision at all for the demanding terrain following regime, and while engine starts were on target – they could hardly be otherwise – the number of shutdowns was too low by a factor of 4. A number of revisions to the programme were obviously needed.

Realistic test schedule

The first step was to provide a test schedule which truly reflected the B-1's operational cycle. A start was made by isolating those areas of the flight regime which make the greatest demands on the engines. These were found to be hot running, which in operational usage tends to gradually increase until red line limits are reached; throttle transients, which are experienced in rapid accelerations and decelerations and in the case of the B-1 occurred during overshoots on landing and touch-and-go training; the throttle juggling involved in terrain-following flight and in-flight refuelling; high cycle fatigue resonance; and start-up and shutdown. Rather surprisingly, shutdown was found to be almost as bad as start-up, especially if maximum operating conditions had been reached during the test, due to the wide variation in temperatures experienced. At the other end of the scale, the less demanding areas were taxiing, cruising, landing approach, and time spent on station throttled back for maximum endurance.

Once these criteria were established, the next step was to revise the test schedule on a more realistic basis. The first decision was to double the initial operational TBO specification needs to provide an endurance test equivalent to

Left: In-flight refuelling is an integral part of the B-1 mission, and either the Air Force flying boom shown in operation here or the US Navy drogue system can be used.

Below: An intimate rear view of the F101-GE-102 reveals details of the 12-segment variable nozzle and the 28-chute mixed flow augmentor. The flameholders are in the centre.

up was despatched to Rockwell International during the following October. GE began testing the core engine on October 29, some 17 days ahead of schedule, and the first complete engine to be fitted with the afterburner was tested during the following April, achieving 90 per cent of its rated speed.

The YF101 development engine passed its Critical Design Review in July 1972, and the first engine was delivered to Rockwell International for installation trials 11 months later. The first flight test YF101 was delivered on March 22, 1974, immediately after the successful completion of the Preliminary Flight Rating Test (PFRT), and a further three engines for the first B-1 prototype had arrived by mid-May. Also tested was the ability of the secondary power system to start all four engines simultaneously while pro-

General Electric F101-GE-102 turbofan

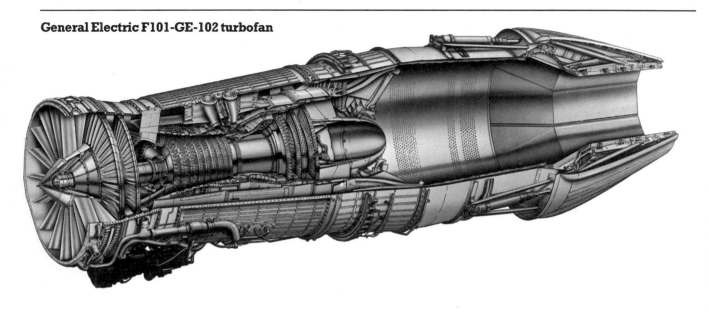

1,000 hours. Secondly, with the exception of the high cycle fatigue resonance conditions, all the more demanding areas would be reproduced on a one-for-one basis, while terrain-following transients were to be included.

These recommendations were adopted, with the result that the 300-hour Product Verification test included some 200 starts and shutdowns and 440 throttle transients, while 225 hours of the 300 were devoted to climb and terrain-following flight regimes, representing the demanding parts of 200 five-hour missions.

A further recommendation was for the adoption of a Continued Engineering Development (CED) programme. Previously the QT had been accepted as qualifying an engine for mass production, but CED was intended to use early production engines to uncover problems early, rather than to wait for them to occur during operational service, and included logistics and maintenance in addition to actual operational experience. The critical design review was approved by the USAF in July 1975, PV was completed, and CED commenced in August 1976. The production decision was made in November of that year, and a production contract issued to GE, who at this point had built a total of 46 YF101 engines, of which 23 had been delivered to Rockwell International.

The cancellation of the B-1A by the Carter Administration in June 1977 put the F101 programme on the backburner, and CED continued through to March 1981, shortly before the B-1 flight test programme ground to a halt, when roughly 7,600 flying hours had been recorded on the four B-1As. The intention was threefold: engine maturity had to be established, component life extended and engine procurement and running costs reduced. It should be remembered in this context that the F101DFE, with an identical core engine to the -100, was under development, and at the same time there was a groundswell of optimism that the B-1 would one day be resurrected.

This optimism was not misplaced; in September 1981 a Presidential go-ahead was received for the B-1B, to be powered by the F101-102. The -102 was almost identical to the -100, but with the accent on durability and operability, and the proposed weight increase for the B-1B required rather higher turbine temperatures to maximize performance and improve operating efficiency. Other changes were neutral installation, so that any engine could be installed in any position, and a simplified nozzle, while the intakes could also be greatly modified with the relaxation of the Mach 2 speed requirement.

The F101-102 was the first engine to utilize Accelerated Mission Testing (AMT) as a tool for product verification, the latter being completed in February 1982. Two 381-cycle AMT blocks run on

**Centre left: The F101-GE-102 is
somewhat larger than a typical fighter
engine, partly because its greater
bypass ratio calls for a fan of greater
diameter. It is giving more thrust than
expected.**

**Left: This view shows clearly the rear
nacelle details of the first production
B-1B during preparations for a test
flight. Details of the main gear are also
visible, as is the unusual cross-section
of the main gear well doors.**

a -102 during its PV programme involved some 790 hours of running time, more than half of which was at full thrust, including 4,713 afterburner lightups, 830 low fatigue cycles and 9,427 full thermal cycles – a rough equivalent of ten years of service usage. PV was complete by February 1982, and the production contract, worth $182 million, was received by GE on April 1 of the same year.

Full scale development was completed during September 1983, and the first production -102 engine was delivered that same month, taking to the air aboard the first B-1B in October 1984. At a casual glance the -102 is identical to the -100, and its dimensions are the same, but it is about 400lb (180kg) heavier. Extremely reliable in service, it is reportedly very stall-proof, and early shortcomings found in sfc were fairly marginal – between 3 and 5 per cent – and were deemed to be acceptable.

The F101 in detail

The F101 is a two-spool turbofan with a bypass ratio of roughly 2 and a mass flow of approximately 350lb (160kg) of air per second. Overall dimensions are identical for both the -100 and the -102, length being 15.08ft (4.60m) and maximum diameter 4.58ft (1.40m), but while the dry weight of the -100 is approximately 4,000lb (1,814kg), the -102 shows an increase, mainly due to improved durability, to 4,400lb (1,996kg). Each produces the same static thrust at military and augmented settings of 17,000lb (75.6kN) and 30,000lb (133.4kN), although the actual flight performance of the -102 is rather the better of the two, as one would expect, being the latest development of a design nearly 20 years old. The F101 is modular, which assists maintenance and repair, and has many borescope ports to allow visual inspection of such areas as the compressor, the combustors, and the turbine, particularly the compressor and turbine blade clearances.

The low-pressure (LP) compressor is the two-stage fan, which also has inlet guide vanes with variable trailing edge flaps. Originally both fan stages had solid titanium blades with tip shrouds for improved clearance control, but in the -102, the first stage LP fan blades are made of a directionally solidified DSR80H nickel based alloy, and the front frame and fan section have been amended due to the adoption of fixed inlets on the B-1B. This, combined with other improvements led GE to anticipate a 17°C temperature improvement and 2½ per cent more thrust: in fact, they got a 33°C improvement in temperature and 5 per cent extra thrust. The effect on takeoff performance was dramatic, the B-1B lifting off five seconds earlier than with the -101. The fan casing is designed to split horizontally for ease of maintenance, allowing the individual vanes and blades to be replaced as required, and the shroud was designed with a short chord as a weight reduction measure.

The outer fan duct is a separate module, and it directs the bypass air around the core engine. The first module in the core engine is the high pressure (HP) compressor, which incorporates high stage loading from the earlier X370

Above right: Ground testing for high altitude, high speed operation is carried out in a test cell which can simulate the conditions required at Air Force Systems Command's Arnold Engineering Development Center.

Right: The shrouds surrounding the afterburner section can be seen in this study of the starboard engines being fitted to the seventh B-1B. The exhaust nozzles of the F101-102 were simplified to save weight.

engine, and a cooled aft casing provides blade clearance control. Like the fan casing, the HP compressor casing splits horizontally for access, the front section being made of titanium and the rear section of steel. The compressor itself has nine stages, the first three of which have variable stators, and the rotor is fabricated by inertia-welding the separate rotor discs together to form a rigid steel drum.

Behind the HP compressor comes the heart of the engine, the combustor, in which the fuel is mixed with air and burnt to produce power. The first machined ring type combustor used in a high performance engine, it is a short annular type with fuel injected through dual cone nozzles into the dome area scroll cups for ignition. This gives a uniform temperature distribution at the HP turbine nozzle, through its ability to mix fuel and air over a very short distance.

Next in line comes the HP turbine, which drives the HP compressor by way of a concentric outer shaft, and has but a single stage with 85 blades. The turbine disc forging was originally to be Rene 120, a development by GE in the powder metallurgy field, but this gave trouble and its replacement, Rene 95, was also unsatisfactory in the early stages, so the -102 uses DA718 nickel alloy in both the turbine and compressor discs. The problem was finally solved by adding an extrusion step prior to forging, and using an improved Rene 95 alloy. The HP turbine blades and vanes are hollow aerofoils with compressor air cooling through film holes on the rear edge of the blades, and the inclusion of more film holes on the back edge of the blades is stated to reduce temperatures at the trailing edges by as much as 110°C. In the -102, the blades are made of directionally solidified DSR80H nickel based alloy. Since 1982 lasers have been used to drill these holes. This is a cleaner and faster

process than either electro-discharge machining or electro-steam drilling, the methods that were used previously. This cooling system makes the expansion characteristics compatible with those of the rotor, which aids control of tip clearances.

Just behind the HP turbine is the LP turbine, which drives the fan through a central shaft or spool. A two-stage design, it is uncooled and has shrouded tips to the blades. The LP turbine blades are individually replaceable, but the second stage vanes are only replaceable in segmented groups. The LP turbine is immediately ahead of the afterburner, or strictly speaking for a turbofan engine, the augmentor.

The augmentor is of the mixed flow type, with 28 chutes handling the core exhaust gases and a further 28 to carry bypass air. A convoluted flow mixer provides for the efficient mingling of the two air sources in the plane of the

Above: To achieve speeds in excess of Mach 2 an external shock inlet was adopted for the B-1A. The three-piece vertically aligned ramp is in the centre and the variable inlet lips can be seen in the open position which is adopted for takeoff.

flameholders, which are radial, and are sited in the hot core exhaust, which is the best place for both lighting up and stable high-altitude operation.

Augmentor operation is electronically controlled, and a self-balancing cycle for the airflow mix is incorporated. One of the considerations in determining this cycle was the reduction of infra-red signature, although no specific details have been released. Augmentation operation is reported to be very smooth, and completely variable over the entire range. Light-up begins on the inner flameholder and works progressively outward; GE have stated that about nine-tenths of the core exhaust is burned before the oxygen-rich bypass air is used. This helps to even out the rise in temperature as increasing amounts of fuel are fed into the augmentor. The augmentor liner is cooled by bypass air.

At the extreme end of the engine comes the nozzle, which is naturally a convergent-divergent type made up of primary and divergent leaves with outer flaps and seals. Optimum area for each flight condition is achieved by means of a translating actuator ring which adjusts the flaps and seals by way of cams and links; the actuator ring is moved by hydraulic rams. Trouble was experienced with the nozzle during the early flight test phase when several leaves were shed at high speeds and altitudes, and a certain amount of redesign was necessary to cure the problem.

Nacelle installation

The engines are housed in pairs in nacelles under the wing root, and although the nacelles are widely spaced flight testing has established that the failure of both engines in one nacelle, although causing asymmetric thrust, will not cause undue control problems. The Automatic Flight Control System (AFCS) will compensate aerodynamically for any potential yaw arising from this condition. The B-1B can even be flown on one engine, although fuel must be jettisoned to lighten the aircraft to acceptable levels.

Rapid starting is essential to survive a surprise attack, and the externally powered electric starter originally con-

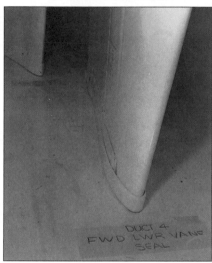

Above: In order to help shield the engine face from the emissions of hostile radars, the vertical inlet guide vanes have been repositioned at various angles to deflect the impulses, as seen here.

sidered was rejected because of its vulnerability to EMP. Orthodox start carts would have reduced stand-alone capability, and in any case were not really conducive to a rapid escape from a threatened airfield. Instead, a gas turbine Auxiliary Power Unit (APU) in each nacelle has a power shaft to each engine, coupled through a gear box.

The APU not only provides power to start the engines: each engine in a nacelle can be started simultaneously with the other using low pressure air; alternatively either APU can start the engines in the opposite nacelle; but power and bleed air are provided for static ground operation. The engines themselves provide power for all hydraulic and electrical systems, plus bleed air for the environmental control system. The B-1B is rather quicker to start than the B-1A; in the event of an alert, the first crew member to reach the foot of the access ladder hits a switch mounted on the nosegear, and by the time the crew reach their stations, both APUs are running and power is reaching all systems. All four engines can then be started simultaneously.

The front of the nacelle contains the intakes, and these have changed considerably during the development period, as the original requirement for Mach 2 performance at altitude with the B-1A was dropped in favour of greater stealth on the B-1B. Early in the B-1A's development a highly efficient but rather

B-1B intake layout

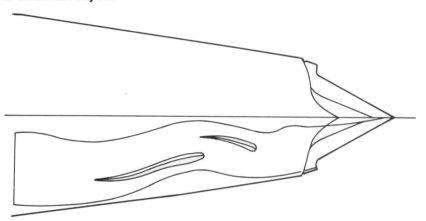

Above: Low observables technology has been applied to the intakes, resulting in a serpentine duct with angled guide vanes and baffles to deflect or trap radar energy. Heated vanes are shown in red.

Below: The B-1B intake is quite different from that of the B-1A, (top left). A plain intake with no variable ramp, it retains the movable lips which are needed to increase air ingestion at takeoff.

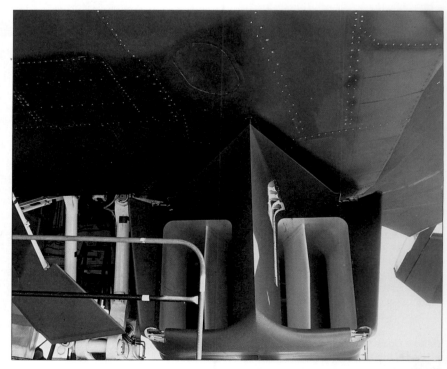

complicated mixed external and internal shock system was considered, but this was abandoned after cost-effectiveness studies, and a slightly less efficient external shock system was adopted.

Regardless of the speed of the aircraft, air entering the engines must be slowed to subsonic speed before it reaches the face of the LP compressor, and setting up a shock wave or a series of shock

waves is the best way of doing this. The inlets are raked back sharply as on many modern fighters, but they are aligned horizontally instead of vertically. The main ramp on the B-1A was therefore vertically aligned, and consisted of three hinged panels, hydraulically actuated and controlled by computer, and the first and third panels, the ramp and the throat, move independently as a function

Powerplant

Left: A closeup of the front of a B-1B engine nacelle, showing how well the engine compressor face is shielded from hostile radar emissions. In this pre-installation picture, the variable lips are constricted into a normal in-flight position.

Right: The B-1B achieves its intercontinental range by carrying an enormous load of fuel, which is distributed around the aircraft as shown here. The centre of gravity is maintained by automatically transferring fuel from tank to tank.

B-1B fuel stowage

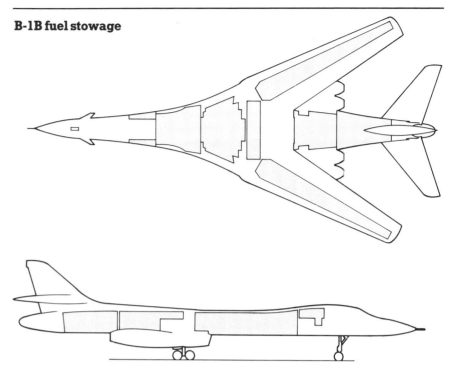

of the Mach number. Basically they remain collapsed, or fixed, at Mach numbers up to about 1.4. At takeoff, the inlet lip moves outward to increase the mass air flow. Boundary layer control in supersonic flight is achieved by the use of two-position louvres on the underside of the nacelle, while the Mach number in the duct diffuser is controlled automatically using a bypass door just ahead of the engine face.

Given the present state of the art, bisonic speed and stealth are mutually exclusive. Mach 2 is only achieved at high altitudes in full view of enemy radar; afterburning greatly increases the aircraft's IR signature; and the inlet design allows radar to look straight down the intake to the face of the engine. The rapidly rotating compressor blades are excellent radar reflectors; since there is always at least one blade at the exact angle to bat the electromagnetic pulse straight back on a reciprocal course, which is exactly what is not wanted if the aircraft is to escape detection The engine face can only be shielded from the emissions by an inlet that precludes Mach 2 speeds.

With the accent on stealth, the B-1B mission profile altered somewhat. Range could be given by high altitude economical cruise in friendly or neutral environments, but the growing difficulty of successfully carrying out a mission involving a deep penetration of hostile airspace placed the highest premium on remaining undetected. Mach 2 at altitude thus became of little importance, while stealthy low-level penetration for protracted periods became an absolute essential.

To reduce the radar signature of the B-1B the intake ducts were made serpentine to prevent hostile radars looking straight down the throat of the engine, vertical inlet guide vanes were repositioned at an angle, and baffles

were inserted to deflect electromagnetic impulses on a winding course both on their way down the intake duct and on their return journey. Extensive use was also made of radar-absorbent materials, so that while radar pulses can still enter the intake, they are either absorbed or deflected downwards, amounting to a tremendous reduction in the B-1B's radar cross section.

Intake simplification

The complicated system of moving ramps and electronic controls on the original B-1A intake would have been self-defeating, and these have been deleted from the B-1B along with the Mach 2 capability, and maximum speed at altitude is now somewhere in the region of Mach 1.3-1.4, but since the supersonic flight regime is considered of little consequence, it is difficult to see exactly where it will fit into the revised mission profile. Invisibility is always better than high performance, though it has been noted that should the USAF ever have a requirement for an ultra long-range interceptor, the original intakes could be fitted to restore the Mach 2 capability.

The B-1B is packed full of fuel. While exact figures have not been released, simple arithmetic gives an approximate figure of 32,000 US gallons, or around 93 tons, carried in eight tanks in the fuselage, in the blended wing body and in the wings, while the forward weapons bays are plumbed for auxiliary tanks. Needless to say, simply leaving all this fuel to slosh around under the influence of gravity would upset the balance of the aircraft, and it will be remembered that an out-of-balance condition led to the loss of the third prototype. Matters are further complicated by the variable-sweep wing, which also alters the centre of gravity.

The answer lies in the Fuel and Center

of Gravity Management Subsystem (FCGMS), which automatically maintains balance by pumping fuel around the tanks. It measures the fuel weight in each tank, then combines this information with weapon load data from the stores management system, and the under-carriage, flaps and wing sweep position, Mach number, pressure altitude and aircraft attitude, and from this calculates the actual centre of gravity. The FCGMS then compares this data with stored moment arm data, and if an out-of-balance condition exists it gives control signals which open and close valves and start and stop fuel pumps to transfer fuel around the system to achieve a balanced flight condition. Pressure in the tanks is maintained by pumping nitrogen in through the vent subsystem, which also prevents the buildup of an explosive fuel vapour/air mixture.

There are two separate main tanks, and each has two booster pumps and one cooling fuel pump. These supply fuel to the engines and to two cooling fuel

loops, while cross-feed valves permit the supply of fuel to all four engines from either tank. The cooling loops are used to regulate the temperatures of the accessory drive gearbox, the avionics bays, the oil for the hydraulic systems and the integrated drive generator by way of environmental control heat exchangers. Fuel is also supplied to the APU in each nacelle, enabling the APU and cooling systems to operate during ground alert status. Fuel transfer can also be operated manually from the cockpit, where a fuel management panel is fitted. In the main, fuel transfer is a fore-and-aft operation, with a separate line and isolation valve providing unobstructed flow between the front and rear fuselage tanks.

Below: The operational pre-flight scene will be much more spartan, as the B-1B will deploy to small fields for periods of 30 days, depending entirely on its own resources once it has topped up with fuel.

Avionics and Armament

To enable it to carry out its design role of penetrating the most intense defences to deliver nuclear weapons, day or night and in any weather, the B-1B carries two comprehensive suites of avionics, one offensive and the other defensive in character and each with its own specialist operator. Many details of these systems are highly classified, and it is impossible to give a comprehensive account of their operation; moreover, the hiatus between the cancellation of the B-1A in 1977 and its reinstatement as the B-1B in late 1981 allowed many technological improvements to be incorporated into the later aircraft's systems, and in some areas there is little similarity between the two.

Above: Not the B-1B impersonating the Space Shuttle, but an avionics test rig for the antenna systems. Some idea of the importance of the avionics can be gained by the extreme lengths and cost to which the USAF and contractors have obviously gone.

From the outset, defining the avionics needs of the B-1 was seen to be a major task. It was originally proposed to keep costs down by assembling a suite of off-the-shelf avionic subsystems tied together with a central complex of computers, but it was soon realized that development and integration would be both expensive and technically risky, so it was decided to assemble the highly specialized defensive avionics suite as a separate package.

Rockwell International and General Electric were selected as weapon system and engine contractors respectively in June 1970, but selection of the avionic system contractors was delayed while proposals were evaluated. Boeing Military Airplane Company (BMAC) were eventually nominated for the offensive avionics system (OAS) in April 1972, while the AIL Division of Cutler-Hammer, now the Eaton Corporation, was not appointed to develop the defensive avionics system (DAS) until January 1974 – less than a year before the maiden flight of the first B-1A.

Although two separate contractors were concerned with the main B-1 avionic systems, and there were certain flight control and other systems that lay outside the scope of either of them, the avionics suite has to be interdependent and operate as part of a cohesive whole and there are parts of the system which are either integrated with both the OAS and the DAS, or which have multiple functions within the electronic innards of the aircraft.

At the heart of the B-1 avionic systems are four redundant MIL-STD-1553 data buses, which have replaced the avionics multiplex (AMUX) system used in the B-1A. A data bus can be considered as a single-track loop railway with many

Below left: The pilot's console is dominated by the central CRT, which in this instance apparently shows the aircraft to be in a gentle left turn at low level. There is no HUD, but the CRT is set only just below the pilot's normal line of vision.

other lines leading off it: information is fed into the loop from one of the lines, and coded so that it is automatically taken off at the appropriate intersection. The data buses sort information from the radars, navigation, flight monitoring systems and so on and feed it to the relevant compartments.

If the data buses are at the heart of the system, then electronic multiplexing (EMUX) forms the arteries, using only two two-wire cables to transfer more than 9,000 inputs and outputs selectively, from any point in the aircraft to any other point via a common data bus. Routing is

done via a controller/processor which can also solve combined sequence or interlocking equations and from them produce output commands. EMUX saves a colossal amount of wiring – some 32,000 wire segments with a total length of 80 miles (129km) – a great deal of complexity, and some 3,000lb (1,360kg) in weight.

Onboard test system

Vital to the efficient operation of the B-1 is the Central Integrated Test System (CITS). This is an onboard digital data processing system which continually

monitors and verifies the performance of various parts of the system, both in flight and on the ground, including offensive and defensive avionic systems, the AFCS and the powerplant, recording in-flight failures and battle damage, and, although almost all systems have a measure of redundancy built in, projecting the systems status onto a display in the centre of the avionics panel. CITS uses an IBM AP101F computer for monitoring and programming, and a program is presently under development to augment its capabilities still further by adding an Expert Parameter

Above left: There are remarkably few instruments in front of the pilot, and only one old-fashioned dial type to be seen from here.

Above: The co-pilot's station is almost identical to that of the pilot. Only the side console and the wing sweep control are handed.

Below: The flight controls are more like those of a fighter, with the stick-type control column and the quadruple throttles set under the left hand in both positions.

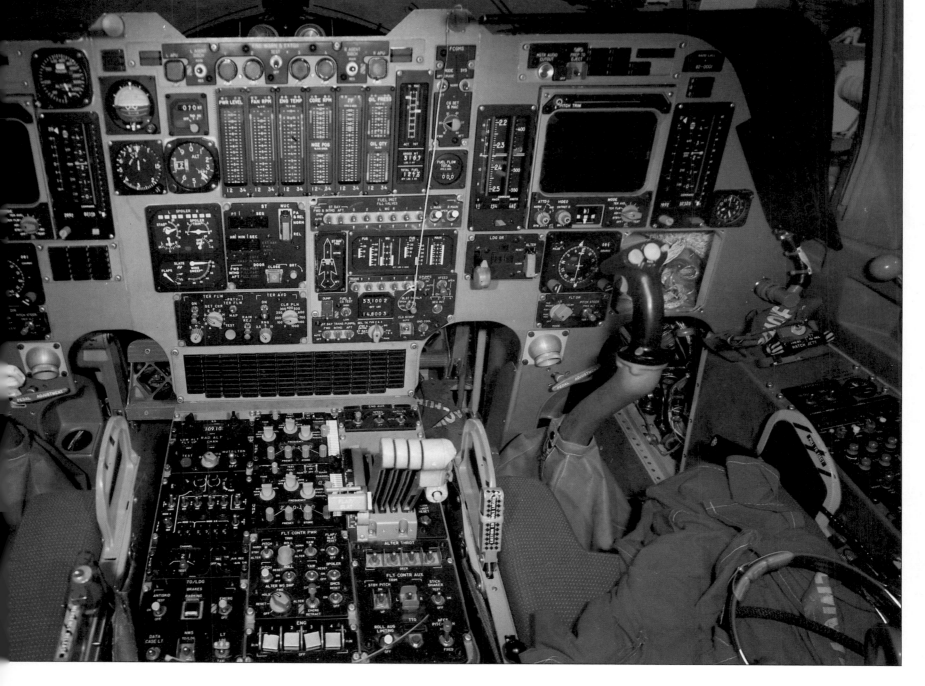

Avionic systems control console

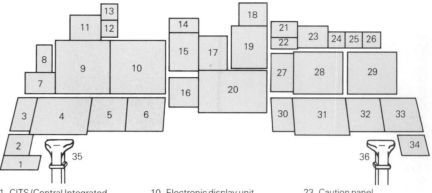

1 CITS (Central Integrated Test System)
2 Lights
3 DSO (Defensive Systems Operator) power
4 Multi-function display
5 Integrated keyboard
6 ALQ-161 RFS/ECM (Radio Frequency Surveillance/Electronic Countermeasures)
7 ICS (Integrated Communications System)
8 Environmental controls
9 Electronic display unit (EDU)
10 Electronic display unit (EDU)
11 Caution panel
12 Attitude/director indicator
13 Flight performance
14 High frequency radio
15 AFSATCOM (Air Force Satellite Communications) printer
16 AFSATCOM keyboard
17 AFSATCOM control panel
18 Lights
19 Naviation auxiliary panel
20 CITS
21 Coded switch panel
22 Transponder
23 Caution panel
24 Flight performance
25 Attitude/director indicator
26 Horizontal situation indicator
27 Bomb/navigation panel
28 Radar display unit
29 Multi-function display
30 Radar control panel
31 Multi-function display
32 Integrated keyboard
33 Stores management system
34 ICS
35 DSO tracking handle
36 OSO tracking handle

System called CITEPS, which will more accurately diagnose faults using artificial intelligence software. The self-testing facilities can also detect EMUX failures and bypass the affected areas using redundant circuitry or boxes.

Power for the avionic systems is supplied by three integrated drive generators rated at 105/110kVA, while one single essential bus for the Central Air Data Computer (CADC) can be driven by an emergency 15kVA generator. This is needed particularly for the AFCS which, being tied into virtually everything to do with controlling the aircraft in the air, makes an invaluable contribution to relieving stress on the airframe, particularly in the terrain-following mode, and extending its operational life. As well as terrain following the AFCS provides flight path, airspeed, altitude, automatic throttle operation, roll attitude and Mach holds.

The flight director panel can also be used to establish heading hold, navigation and automatic approach modes, but as we saw in the Structure chapter its most valuable contribution is in damping out gust response. The AFCS has 11 Systron Donner servo/accelerometer packages distributed around the aircraft, containing a total of 27 individual inertial sensors. These monitor the linear acceleration in both vertical and horizontal planes, while providing angular rate inputs about all three axes of motion to the stability and control augmentation system. Extra packs also give lateral and vertical axes plus linear acceleration inputs to the automatic flight controls, and further contributions come from flight director computers and the military avionics systems.

The B-1B OAS differs considerably from that of the B-1A and nowhere more than in the radar fit. The B-1A carried two radars in the nose: the General Electric APQ-144 scanning radar, used for ground mapping and to obtain positional fixes for navigation, target location and weapons targeting; and the Texas Instruments APQ-146 terrain-following radar, both of which were derived from similar items used on the F-111. Both were replaced on the B-1B by the Westinghouse APQ-164 multimode radar which could be used for all these tasks and more besides.

The change stemmed partly from improved technology and partly from the need to reduce observables, and the APQ-164 was derived from the APG-66 fighter radar as used in the F-16, and the USAF Electronically Agile Radar re-

Above: At the heart of the OAS is the APQ-164 radar, the antenna of which is shown here during system integration. The black assembly on the mounting frame is a dummy load for testing without radiation.

Above right: The avionic systems operators' consoles are dominated by three CRT displays each side on which information is presented. While the systems are highly automated, the operators retain overall control through the integrated keyboards.

Right: The phased array antenna of the APQ-164 radar is canted down to reduce its radar reflectivity. Although in this picture it looks movable, it is fixed, and the radar beam is steered and pointed as required by electronic means.

Below: The baseline configuration for B-1B avionics is divided into five interacting parts. Many existing units are incorporated along with several entirely new ones, all linked by a quadruple MIL-STD-1553B EMUX (electronic multiplex) bus.

Avionic system baseline configuration

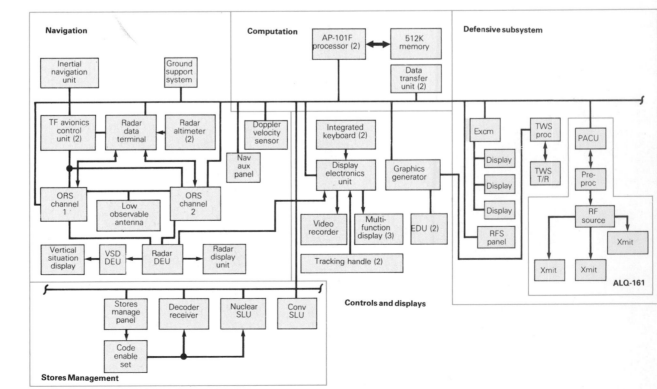

Left: The offensive avionic system
operator's station and, below the CITS
console on the central panel, the
entrance to the tunnel giving access
forward to the flight deck.

search programme, initiated in 1974.
APG-66 technology included the dual
mode transmitter, the Programmable
Signal Processor (PSP), and certain
other components, the resulting com-
monality saving an estimated $350
million, while the EAR programme contributed low-observable phased-array
technology. The APQ-164 was selected
in competition with a hybrid Hughes
radar which combined features of the
APG-63 and APG-65 as used in the F-15
Eagle and F-18 Hornet respectively.

APQ-164 is a dual-channel multimode
coherent pulse-Doppler radar with a low
observable antenna. The dual channel is
used to provide systems redundancy
and only one channel is actively used,
the other being purely a backup. Unlike
previous radars it has a fixed instead of a
moving antenna and scanning is carried
out electronically by the phased array, a
feasible procedure because the scanning angles needed by a fighter radar
are not required, and the angular variation can be more restricted. The antenna
is pointed down, which helps reduce its
radar return, as emissions from hostile
radars will tend to be deflected downward rather than straight back on a reciprocal bearing. It is reported that its
reflectivity to hostile radars is about two
orders of magnitude less from the critical
elevation and direction than were the
two antenna carried by the B-1A.

APQ-164 operating modes

Recent information credits APQ-164
with 13 modes – real beam and high
resolution ground mapping, terrain following, terrain avoidance, Doppler
velocity up-date, rendezvous for in-flight
refuelling, ground moving target indication and ground moving target track,
weather detection and avoidance,
ground or air beacon, monopulse
measurement, and high altitude calibration. The two most important for the B-1B
mission are likely to be ground mapping,
which will be used for route navigation,
updating waypoints, target location and
attack, and terrain following.

Real beam mapping uses low pulse
repetition frequency (prf) combined
with non-coherent pulse-to-pulse frequency hopping (which avoids glint) to
produce a small-scale radar map of the
terrain ahead. This is good enough to
identify large natural features such as
lakes, although it does not have the definition to cope with small natural or man-
made features. It is computer adjusted to
give a vertical map presentation on the
radar screen, thus avoiding the possibility of misidentification of features due
to slant distortion. Doppler beam sharpening can be used to give better definition over smaller areas, but the degree
and ratios have not been released.

For really high resolution ground
mapping, synthetic aperture radar
(SAR) mode is used, and the definition
provided is reported to be as good as
low grade photography. The antenna
can scan through any quadrant between
20° and 60° to either side of the aircraft's
velocity vector – its mean course, taking
into account drift and course corrections
– and SAR works by receiving and processing the returning radar emissions
over "a significant distance", which is the
distance travelled by the B-1B during a

Left: OAS simulator in operation. A
ground map is visible on the radar
display unit, while alpha-numeric
information is presented on the two
multi-function displays.

set time. During this time the velocity of the radar returns from each particular point being illuminated alters in direct relationship to the changing angle; in other words, as the aircraft moves, so the angle to each individual point, and with it the characteristics of the radar reflection, alters. The general effect is that of having a radar antenna many hundreds of feet wide – wide enough, in fact, to present angular variation information. Further processing is then carried out to give a precise fixing for navigation updating, or an attacking solution for a target.

SAR is not new technology; it was first developed in the 1960s for reconnaissance purposes, but only in fairly recent times did the means become available for the extraction and presentation of radar data to permit targeting. The definition of SAR imagery on the B-1B is said to be so good that it will allow a landing on a damaged airfield at night or in bad weather without recourse to ground based landing aids, always supposing that enough concrete remains. The full capabilities of SAR have not yet been released, but it seems reasonable to suppose that many functions will be enhanced by its use, apart from navigation and target acquisition.

When using either SAR or real beam mapping modes, the radar presents the picture on the radar display, or alternatively on one of the multi-function displays (MFDs) in the offensive avionics systems operator's position (the right-hand seat). When it becomes necessary to update the navigation via a pre-programmed waypoint, the display will place

cross-hairs over the calculated position, and any deviation will show up as a displacement against the real point which will be depicted on the screen. The operator, via a tracking handle, then moves the cross-hairs to the exact spot, which automatically updates the navigation system and puts the aircraft precisely on track.

Terrain following modes

Terrain following is accomplished in a combination of three modes – hard, medium and soft – and any one of 11 ground clearance altitudes, the lowest of which is believed to be 200ft (60m) or less, selected according to the demands of the mission, the nature of the terrain to be traversed and the degree of threat. Obviously, in a high threat area hard ride and a low altitude will be optimum, but despite the low gust response of the B-1B and the smoothing effect of the SMCS system, prolonged flight in these conditions would be tiring, and would lower crew efficiency, so where it is reasonable to do so, a compromise solution is likely to be adopted between the demands of security and crew comfort.

Terrain-following radar scanning is not a continuous process, since although the beam is narrow, and fairly difficult to acquire by hostile monitoring stations, it is still an emission and thus subject to possible detection. Instead, a guidance algorithm developed by Boeing is used to compute the required flight path from the scan signal returns, and this also calculates when another scan should be made. The radar emissions are therefore intermittent rather than constant, making

them more difficult to detect, especially over flat terrain where the intervals between scans will be less frequent than over hilly country. The flight path is scanned in a range/altitude profile out to roughly 10nm (18.5km) and the data passed to the radar and navigational computers, which calculate the flight profile to be followed and transmit the data to the terrain following control unit, which feeds commands into the flight control system.

Terrain avoidance, on the other hand, simply warns the pilot of obstacles, and it is then up to him to avoid them. Any of the 11 clearance altitudes can be selected according to the nature of the terrain, and the radar scan works to this level. Only obstacles that reach higher than the selected altitude are shown on the pilot's and co-pilot's situation displays whereas in terrain following mode both the flight path and the terrain profile are presented for monitoring.

The OAS contains a total of 66 LRUs of 41 different types, and the complete shipset weighs 2,883lb (1,308kg). In all, 20kVA of power are needed to run it. So far we have considered only the radar, but there many other systems, mainly to do with navigational functions, plus the computer bloc.

Precise navigation over very long distances is essential to the success of the mission, and while the radar modes can help considerably by pinpointing waypoints and geographical features, they are no more than aids. The inertial navigation system (INS), however, is of fundamental importance. The entire route is carefully planned beforehand

Above: The first B-1B in system checkout at Palmdale. Unpainted, the aircraft shows the dielectric panels at the wing root and the base and tip of the fin behind which receivers and transmitters for the ALQ-161 system are located.

and the details preprogrammed onto a cassette tape which is fed into the navigation system.

The INS is precisely aligned before takeoff, or possibly in the air in the event of an emergency scramble, and a complex system of sensors feeds information into the INS during flight, enabling it to keep track of the aircraft's position to a high degree of accuracy. The B-1A carried redundant twin Litton inertial systems, but upgraded requirements for the B-1B, stated as a factor of 2.5 better unaided inertial accuracy, doubled accuracy (or halved error) in weapons release, and a three times more accurate attitude reference for the radar in the terrain following or avoidance modes, called for something better.

The unit chosen was the Singer Kearfott SKN-2440, two of which are installed in the development B-1Bs, although only one is to be carried in operational aircraft; should it be found desirable to retrofit a second, the wiring is already in place. SKN-2440 is a development of the SKN-2416 and SKN-2430 as used on the F-16, and the associated sensors are the Teledyne APN-218 Doppler velocity sensor, which is a modified variant of that used in the B-52, and dual Honeywell APN-224 radar altimeters, also used on the B-52. These items replaced their

ALQ-161 defensive avionic system configuration

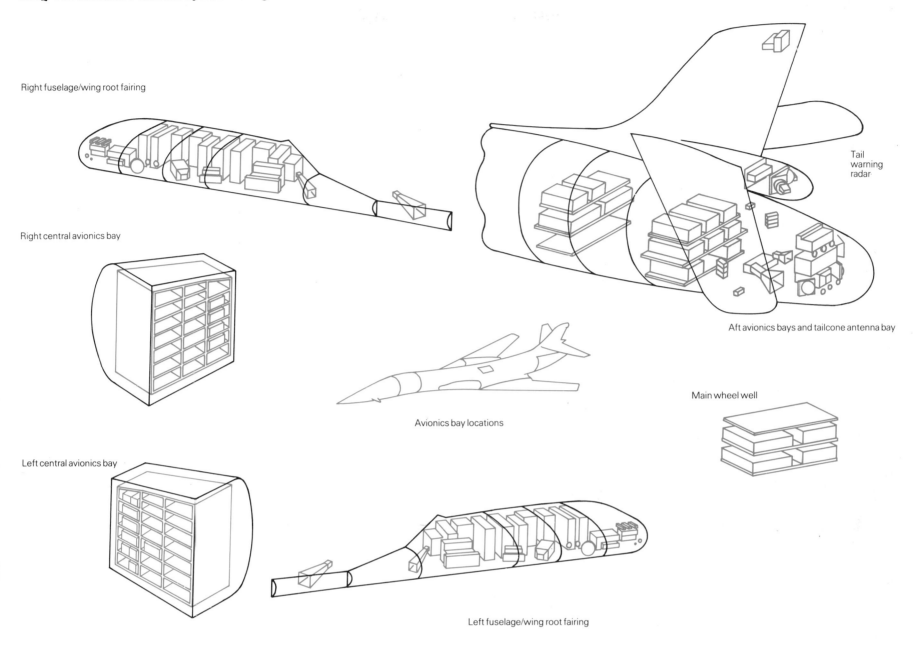

Right fuselage/wing root fairing

Right central avionics bay

Left central avionics bay

Tail warning radar

Aft avionics bays and tailcone antenna bay

Main wheel well

Avionics bay locations

Left fuselage/wing root fairing

Above: The Eaton ALQ-161 defensive avionic system comprises no fewer than 107 separate units dispersed around the aircraft to give comprehensive coverage. It is designed to detect and defeat known and projected threats.

Right: Both the OAS and the DAS are heavily reliant on LRUs, one of which, a component of the ALQ-161, is seen here. Serviceability is greatly eased when a faulty unit can be replaced within minutes by a ground crewman wearing gloves.

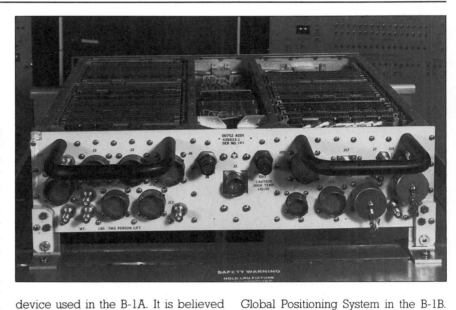

counterparts on the B-1A, whose gimballed Doppler motion sensor was found to be unsatisfactory and was replaced by the non-gimballed Teledyne APN-200 in 1976, and the Honeywell APN-194 radar altimeter.

It was proposed in 1982 to support APN-218 with the Honeywell AAN-131 precision navigation system, but this seems to have been dropped. Other aids proposed for the B-1A were a Hughes forward-looking infra red (FLIR) sensor and a Dalmo-Victor low light television (LLTV), which were to have made up the electro-optical viewing system. In 1976 it was reported that the FLIR was to be hardened against EMP and redesigned for a new location along the aircraft centreline, but this was never implemented, and no electro-optical sensors were scheduled for the B-1B by early 1986, although Low Altitude Navigation and Targeting Infra Red at Night (Lantirn) may well be incorporated if trials are successful.

Computers play a big part in tying the OAS and its associated systems together. The B-1A used the Singer Kearfott 2070 in the OAS, but in 1976 the USAF directed Boeing to look for a cheaper alternative as part of the design to cost directive. The B-1B uses the IBM AP-101F, a dual architecture computer

compatible with both the MIL-STD-1553 and -1750 databuses, which was developed from the AP-101C as used in the OAS of the B-52, and it was originally anticipated that an updated variant of the B-52 model would be used, but the AP-101F turned out to be different enough to warrant a new designation. The radar incorporates two AP-101Fs dedicated to terrain following, one of which is on the backup system as described earlier. These compare the actual flight path with the calculated flight path and command corrections from the flight control system.

At the very centre of the OAS lie four AP-101Fs, navigation, control and display, and weapons control occupying one each while the fourth serves for backup while monitoring critical functions. All the computers connect with a mass memory unit with a capacity of 512K words, including the AP-101F in the CITS and another in the defensive avionic system. The taped mission instructions are fed into this via two Sundstrand data transfer units, while a mass of information, such as data on known hostile emitter characteristics, is also stored ready to be called up on demand. The memory unit is a development of that used in the B-52 OAS, and uses a core memory rather than the drum storage

device used in the B-1A. It is believed that this unit is slightly more vulnerable to TREES (transient response of electronic equipment and systems), which is the effect of exposure to gamma rays and high energy particles, but that the advantages of the system more than outweigh the disadvantages.

More exotic items apart, the B-1B carries the usual sort of avionics kit one would expect – VHF and HF radios, TACAN, ILS and so on, plus secure voice communications. Most of these have been checked and in some cases modified to give the required degree of EMP and TREES hardening. The B-1A was fitted with the ASC-19 satellite communications set but, rather surprisingly, the Air Force is not planning to fit a satellite signal receiver for the Navstar

Global Positioning System in the B-1B.

Rumour also has it that bistatic radar has been under consideration for the B-1B. This is a type of radar where the transmitter and receiver have separate antennas which in airborne use are mounted on separate illuminator and attacker aircraft. The transmitter, which is announcing its presence to the enemy by its emissions, remains in neutral or friendly airspace, while the receiver homes on the reflected emissions without betraying its presence. Presumably, if bistatic radar were adopted, the B-1B would carry the receiver while a B-52 operating in the stand-off role could carry the transmitter. A test programme was initiated by the USAF in 1980, at which time considerable technical problems remained to be overcome, not the

decoder/receiver provides the interface with the weapons.

The OAS consists of many different subsystems carrying out different functions, but linked together and monitored and controlled primarily by the OAS operator; the Defensive Avionic System (DAS), on the other hand, is a much more cohesive system, a fact reflected in its Air Force systems designation of AN/ALQ-161. ALQ-161 is an advanced system devoted mainly to electronic countermeasures, although some infra-red kit is included. In all, including antennas, black boxes, displays and controls, it totals 107 separate items, of which 52 are unique to the system. Most are LRUs weighing between 40lb and 80lb (18-36kg), easily accessible and very quickly replaceable. Total system weight, excluding cables, displays and control units, is about 5,200lb (2,360kg), and when its full jamming capability is utilized it consumes roughly 120kW of power, the equivalent of 120 microwave ovens working simultaneously.

Defensive avionics

Penetration is central to the primary B-1B mission: remaining undetected is the best aid to penetration, and the low-level terrain-following flight path and the low-observables technology built into the design are steps toward this goal. Even so, undetected penetration could only be assured by silence and invisibility – to radar and infra-red detection as well as to the human eyeball – and there is no way to conceal an aeroplane weighing more than 200 tons. This is where ALQ-161 comes in as a vital second line of defence.

Modern air defence systems are heavily reliant on radar. The human eye can be defeated by the cover of darkness, or by bad weather; the human ear was never much good against even high and slow targets, and the B-1B is certainly not that; and infra-red also has drawbacks as a means of primary detection. All of which leaves radar detection, which can sometimes, although by no means always, be circumvented by low flying and terrain masking. But sooner or later, in a comprehensive defensive radar system, even the low-observable B-1B will be located. The trick then is to conceal not its presence, but its exact location, course, and speed. ALQ-161 uses antennas, located around the airframe to give 360° cover, which can tell when it is being painted by a hostile radar. The system then deploys what amounts to protective electronic camouflage by jamming or deceiving the enemy radars. It cannot conceal its presence by these means – *something* must be there to cause the jamming – but it can conceal its location, identity and purpose from the detection system.

In hardware terms, the ALQ-161 has changed little between the B-1A and the B-1B. Although the computers and the data bus are of improved types with greater capacity, the main improvement comes from programmability. Far more advanced programs are now possible, and full use is being made of them.

ALQ-161 is for all practical purposes fully automatic, with the operator acting as a systems manager, monitoring operations but only actively intervening in circumstances where human judgement is felt to be superior to that of the computer programs. It is anticipated that programming advances will be able to keep pace with the abilities of threat radars for many years to come, with updated software obviating the need for new hardware.

The fourth B-1A featured a dorsal spine extending from just behind the cockpit to the fin. This was connected with an experimental monopulse radar

Electronically steerable transmit antenna

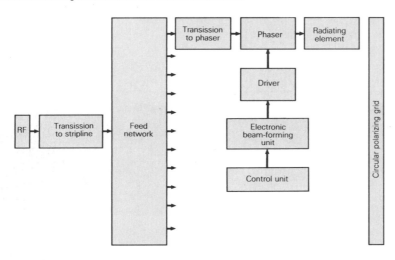

Above: Ergonomic checkout of the DAS console. The two EDUs show the EW environment in graphic form, while tabulated information is presented on the MFD.

Left: The B-1B carries nine of these Sedco Systems antennas, three each for jamming on Bands 6, 7 and 8, with one for each band in each wing root and in the tailcone.

least of which were the ability to compensate for precise relative navigation and motion, and transmitter/receiver geometry. The operational use of bistatic radar by the B-1B appears to involve considerable difficulties, and no official announcements have been made.

Stores management is a separate subsystem within the OAS. Developed from a similar article on the B-52, it provides status information for the systems operator and control for both conventional and nuclear weapons. The weapon status data is provided by logic units mounted on the rotary launchers in the weapons bays and is shown on the OAS operator's MFD. At the same time, it can command signals to the weapons issued from the OAS switch panel via the computer system. As an obvious precaution against finger trouble or accidental release, the release of nuclear weapons demands two man operation, with controls too widely spaced for one man operability – standard procedure where nuclear weapon delivery systems are concerned. One set of switches is located in the front (pilot's) area of the cockpit while the other set is in the systems operators' section, and a quite complicated procedure is involved, a code enabler set being used to obtain two-station consent for release while a

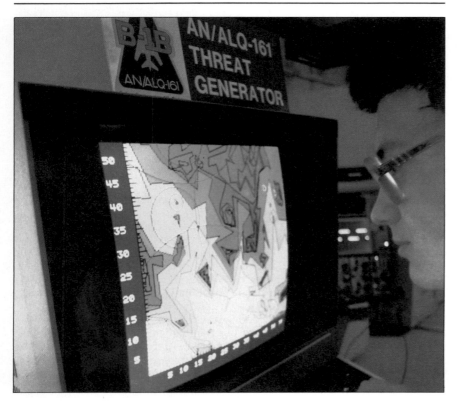

Left: Much of the development work for ALQ-161 was carried out on a simulator – the ALQ-161 Threat Generator, which depicts stylized terrain complete with threats.

ALQ-161 operation

This graphic representation of the ALQ-161's automatic response to detected threats shows threats of increasing frequency from bottom to top and the system's response as time progresses from left to right. The high-priority threat in the top row and the area surveillance radar in the row below are jammed (indicated by the box) until the system has ceased to receive transmissions, as is the high-priority radar in the third row. To deal with the two frequency-hopping radars in the fourth and sixth rows the jammer must transmit over a broader frequency band – using spot jamming against the former and a pulse repeat-back technique against the latter, which covers a wider range – and when a new high-priority threat of undetermined characteristics is detected (bottom row) the frequency-hopping area surveillance radar is left unjammed temporarily to allow power to be concentrated on continuous jamming of the new threat until its scan and pulse rate and other characteristics can be assessed and output can be matched to the individual pulses. Jamming of the continuous-wave radar is also interrupted when the system has to cope with the unclassified threat and the high-priority frequency-hopper, and again when pulses from the two remaining high-priority threats coincide. High-threat emitters would be those associated with AA systems.

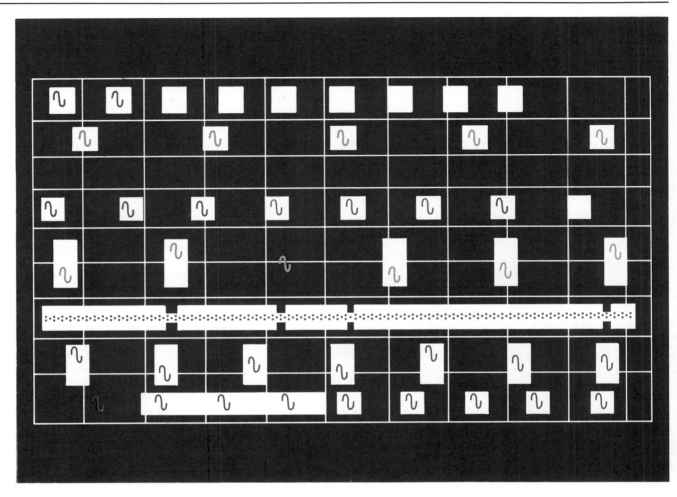

⌐ High-priority radar   ⌐ Area surveillance radar   ∷∷∷ Continuous-wave radar

jamming system called Cross-Eye, developed by Kuras-Alterman, and housed a waveguide; little has been published on it, and it is not carried by the B-1B. The latter does, however, carry the Westinghouse ALQ-153 tail warning radar, the function of which is to detect both aircraft and missiles approaching from astern. As this is an emitter, it would appear to contradict the purpose of ALQ-161 by giving hostile defences something to track, but it is the only piece of equipment able to give warning of, say, a fighter making a visual, no-radar attack from this quarter, and will probably only be used in circumstances where a high risk of such an attack exists.

ALQ-161's operational sequence is listen, detect, classify, establish priority and activate countermeasures. Listening and detection is carried out by electronically steered phased array antennas mounted in the leading edges of the wing gloves and in the tail, each covering an arc of 120° in azimuth and 90° in elevation to provide all-round coverage. The band width is believed to range between VHF, which is used by some Soviet early warning and ground control interception radars, and I/J band, which is used by fighters and surface-to-air missiles. The system is designed to work in a very high threat environment, using jamming in near real time against multiple emitters, without becoming overloaded.

ALQ-161 is basically a passive listening system, only resorting to active countermeasures when absolutely necessary. This is a matter for fine judgement, either by the artificial intelligence of the computer program or by the Defensive Systems Officer, who can override the computer program and delay the onset of jamming if the circumstances warrant. For example, a few faint strobes from an early warning radar do not guarantee that the bomber has been detected, and if jamming is initiated too soon, it will simply confirm that something is out there and alert the system.

When the antennas on the B-1B start picking up hostile radar emissions they pass the basic data to the direction and frequency receivers. The directional receiver sorts out a location for the emitters while the computers analyse the frequency data, which includes tracking radar pulse trains and waveforms, enabling the types of emitter to be identified and assigned threat priorities. Near real-time processing is provided by six data buses which receive information from nine high speed computers called Jamming Logic Allocation Units housed in two black boxes referred to as Jam Logic A and Jam Logic B. The system is controlled by a single IBM AP-101F computer.

Speed and co-ordination are the keynotes of ALQ-161. It is impossible for the B-1B to carry enough jamming transmitters to deal with hostile radars on a one-for-one basis, and ECM is managed on a time-share basis, with jamming priority going to the greatest threat. Where possible, jamming emissions are broadcast on a narrow beamwidth to reduce the power necessary, hopping from threat to threat within milliseconds to give the greatest possible coverage. The number of emitters that the jamming transmitter can cope with simultaneously is quite amazing, and this over a wide frequency spectrum. The system is extremely flexible, and even when the jamming transmitters are heavily engaged the detection subsystem can continue to monitor old signals and detect new ones, even when the jammer is working in the same frequency band. ALQ-161 is configured in such a way that antenna pointing, frequency modulation, and activation are all optimized against the threat radars. If a threat radar ceases

Right: An articulated test assembly is used to check the pattern of emissions from ALQ-161 tailcone antennas. The hoist and platform have anechoic shrouds to eliminate unwanted echoes.

B-1B stores configurations

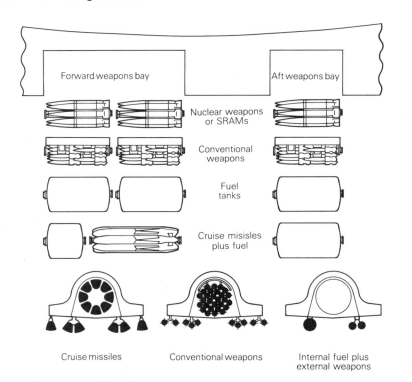

Forward weapons bay | Aft weapons bay

Nuclear weapons or SRAMs

Conventional weapons

Fuel tanks

Cruise misisles plus fuel

Cruise missiles | Conventional weapons | Internal fuel plus external weapons

transmitting, the jamming directed against it is automatically stopped.

The Defensive Systems Officer is kept abreast of the situation via two Sanders CRT displays. One of these is a conventional Plan Position Indicator, which depicts the aircraft and its planned track against a background of threat emitters, which are presented in an alpha-numeric format. The other CRT gives a panoramic picture of the situation with details of the emitters. A cursor can be used to give a more detailed display of any desired area together with a list of both the emitter characteristics and up to five countermeasures modes that can be used aginst it. The DSO can hook in to the system by means of a keyboard if it becomes necessary to take any direct action to modify what ALQ-161 is doing automatically.

The B-1B also carries passive countermeasures in the form of chaff and IR flare decoys. The chaff and flare dispenser is in the top of the fuselage behind the crew compartment, in two rows, with forced ejection of both chaff and flares. Dispensing is automatic, controlled by ALQ-161, or manual, controlled by the DSO, who carefully monitors the supplies remaining at any given moment.

Another feature of ALQ-161 is the monitoring network, Status Evaluation and Test (SEAT), which is linked to the CITS. Any system degradation or failure is overcome by the CITS computer, an IBM AP-101F, which uses a data bus to bypass faulty units and thereby maintain full ECM capability.

Weapons

The weapons load carried by the B-1B is awesome in its destructive power, as the accompanying table shows. Of the nuclear gravity weapons, the B-83 is believed to be considered the primary weapon for the B-1B, with the B-61 a possible alternative, while the B-28 and B-43 are getting rather long in the tooth. The B-83 weighs 2,408lb (1,092kg) and

Left: The movable bulkhead in the forward weapons bay allows ALCMs to be carried. It is unlikely to carry external weapons on missions involving low-level penetration.

Below: SRAMs are loaded onto one of the three rotary launchers that can be carried by the B-1B. Each launcher carries eight missiles for a total internal load of 24.

has a yield of one megaton. Fuzing takes place in flight and can be set for either air or ground burst. It is parachute retarded, and can be dropped from any altitude between 150ft and 50,000ft (46-15,240m), and a new parachute design allows air drops to be made at transonic speeds, and slows the bomb to 60mph (97km/hr). B-61 is a similar but lighter weapon, weighing about 800lb (363kg), and has a yield of between 10 and 500 kilotons.

	Internal	External
Nuclear gravity		
B-28	12	8
B-43	12	14
B-61	24	14
B-83	24	14
Nuclear guided		
AGM-69 SRAM	24	14
AGM-86B ALCM	8	14
Conventional		
Mk 82	84	14
Mk 84	24	14

The Boeing AGM-69 Short Range Attack Missile (SRAM) was developed during the 1960s as a supersonic rocket propelled defence suppression weapon. Both speed and range vary according to the speed and altitude of the launch aircraft, between Mach 2.8 and 3.2, and 35 to 105 miles (56-169km), and warhead yield is 200kT. Production ceased on 1975, but over 1,000 SRAMs remain in the inventory. Once launched it is a difficult weapon to stop, as it has an offset homing ability which enables it even to turn around and strike at a target astern of the launching aircraft.

In 1985 a competition was launched to develop a new short range attack missile, provisionally called SRAM II, to be carried by the B-1B. It is to be smaller than AGM-69 and rocket propelled, and the contending companies are Boeing Aerospace, Martin Marietta Aerospace, and McDonnell Douglas Astronautics. The decision was expected to be made in the first half of 1986, with production of some 1,900 missiles to begin in 1989.

The AGM-86B Air Launched Cruise Missile (ALCM), another Boeing product, played a part in the cancellation of the B-1A when it was thought that it could replace the manned bomber in the penetration role if launched from a stand-off carrier such as the B-52. A jet propelled subsonic missile with a speed of only about 435kt (805km/h), it has a range of some 1,300nm (2,500km) and carries a 200kT warhead. To reach its target it follows a terrain-hugging path using a sophisticated INS and Terrain Contour Matching (Tercom) guidance system, which compares the surface of the area that it is overflying with profiles stored in the computer memory.

The B-1B has also been considered for the maritime surveillance and patrol function. Both the MK-36 and MK-60 sea mine have been mentioned in this connection, while the AGM-84A Harpoon anti-shipping missile is said to be compatible with the B-1B wiring, although certain interface equipment would have to be installed and the correct pylons bolted on.

For self-defence against an air threat, Asraam is the most likely possibility. A short-range, all-aspect heat seeking missile, it would require certain modifications to be made to the OAS, and rails or pylons to be fitted.

While a considerable amount of ordnance can be hung on the outside of the B-1B, this cannot do other than prejudice

Right: The T-38 chase bird keeps a close watch as iron bombs are discharged from the forward weapons bay at fairly low level over the PIRA, located not far from Edwards.

its stealth qualities. For the deep penetration mission, it will probably rely on the content of its vast weapons bays. These contain quick-acting rotary launchers with eight weapons stations on each, and in theory all eight SRAMs on one launcher can be pre-targeted and released within 45 seconds. Undergoing trials at the moment is the Common Strategic Rotary Launcher (CSRL), which will also be used by the B-52. This consists of carbon fibre epoxy tubes 14ft (4.27m) long and 1.75ft (0.53m) in diameter. Aluminium collars at the ends attach the tubes to the aircraft, while six aluminium rings on each tube carry the weapons mounts. A weight saving of some 400lb (181kg) each is achieved by using aluminium instead of steel.

Right: The second prototype B-1 drops an inert B-61 nuclear weapon over the range. The parachute retards the weapon, allowing the fast-flying bomber to evade the explosions.

Below: The B-1 with all weapon bay doors open is an impressive sight, even though only a single bomb is falling. Release and separation appear to have been very clean.

Deployment

The first B-1B was rolled out with due ceremony at Palmdale on September 4, 1985, five months ahead of schedule; the event was greeted by Air Force Secretary Verne Orr with the words, "We don't build bombers to go to war. We build them to keep from going to war. May it never fly in anger." While this laudable sentiment emphasized the deterrent nature of the B-1B, there has been no shortage of attempts to find alternative missions for what is, after all, the world's most expensive military aircraft. It is ironic that one of the alternative roles was described as "a show of force and an expression of national resolve" when the aircraft has been made as near invisible as possible.

At the time of the first B-1B roll-out the first and third B-1A prototypes had been retired from the flight test programme while the second had been lost in a tragic accident. Meanwhile, the fourth B-1A was well along with flight testing the avionic systems in an intensive programme which had started during the previous July and was scheduled to continue for nearly two years, with a total of 380 flying hours, until mid-June 1986, when the official full scale development testing was due to terminate.

At first concentrating on the defensive avionics system, the fourth B-1A's flight programme, carried out from Edwards AFB, allowed flights every Thursday, with every third flight used as a backup to cover the scheduled test points that for one reason or another (and we saw examples of that in the account of the flight that ended in the loss of the second B-1A) had been missed or re-scheduled. High altitude calibration and initial air alignment for weapons release were also carried out by this aircraft.

To expedite the offensive avionics testing, a BAC-111 airliner was fitted out as a flying testbed for the radar systems. This had the advantage that the black boxes could be spread through the fuselage, giving ease of access during flight. The adapted BAC-111 first flew in this role on July 3, 1984, at the start of a year-long programme, concentrating at first on the detailed ground mapping modes.

The first production B-1B joined the flight test programme on October 18, 1984. Fully instrumented for testing such areas as structures, flight control systems and weapons separation, it also carried a fully working offensive avionics system on its first flight, and a considerable proportion of the flight test programme was devoted to working the (unspecified) bugs out of the OAS. The initial emphasis was placed on high resolution ground mapping and fix taking from both high and low altitudes, using synthetic aperture techniques with the radar trained up to 15° sideways. The INS also had to be checked out, and instrument approaches demonstrated in poor visibility with no ground landing aids, using the aircraft's

Above: Originally, the B-1 mission was to involve refuelling after takeoff, but the revised requirement for the B-1B called for the ability to take off with full fuel and continue without support.

on-board systems; and there were some simulated releases of gravity weapons.

For various reasons, which will become apparent, a certain amount of flight testing at very high all-up weights was not possible with this aircraft. Test flight day from Edwards AFB was Wednesday, so as not to clash with the B-1A, and a similar routine of two flights followed by a backup was adopted. In August 1985 the initial production configuration of the ALQ-161

Left: One effect of the European One camouflage scheme is the dramatic changes of colour that occur with changing light conditions: radar may be the main threat, but visual concealment still matters.

Above: KC-135 boom operator's view of the B-1B. The original black markings, seen here, caused the operators severe problems in judging depth while positioning the booms, especially in darkness.

Above: The solution was to add high-visibility white aim pattern markings around the receptacle and on the SMCS vanes, a move which the USAF is satisfied does not affect overall visual signature.

Below: To protect the crew against thermonuclear flash blindness aluminium shields with ceramic portholes are being installed to cover the cockpit transparencies within 150 microseconds.

defensive avionics system was fixed, and shortly afterward the first B-1B was withdrawn from the flight test programme to undergo structural proof loading tests until December of that year. The first SRAM launch had been scheduled for around August or September, but was deferred until after the next aircraft, the ninth production B-1B, joined the test programme.

No 9 is the first machine to incorporate the removable bulkhead between the front weapons bays, and is therefore the first B-1B capable of flying ALCM trials. It was scheduled for delivery on March 15, 1986, and in addition to ALCM and SRAM testing, it will also participate in the testing of flight control, flying qualities and flight at heavy all-up weights.

Below: Escorted by an F-111 and a T-38, the second B-1A prototype releases a SRAM over one of the Edwards weapons ranges during stores separation trials. This drop was made in July 1984.

The 100,000lb (45,360kg) increase in the gross weight of the B-1B compared with the B-1A caused certain problems. The design does not stall in the classic manner where the wings lose lift at a certain combination of speed and angle of attack (AoA), accompanied by wing drop: instead, the aircraft tends to pitch up. The AoA limit is set by the neutral stability of the aircraft, and a Stall Inhibitor System (SIS) was developed to prevent the pilot going past the neutral AoA point by providing a limit in the flight control system with a small built-in safety margin. The SIS has been installed and successfully flown in the first B-1B and is being added to production aircraft on the line from No 10 onwards, and will at some point be retro-

Bottom: The fact that the rocket motor has not ignited indicates that this is a dummy round: the genuine article would already have started the process of accelerating to its top speed of around Mach 3.

fitted to the earlier aircraft.

However, at very heavy weights, flying at the AoA limit imposed by the SIS simply does not give sufficient lift in some flight regimes, and the only answer is to exceed the neutral stability limitations. In order to do this with safety, and in many cases to do so at all, some form of artificial stability must be provided, and a Stability Enhancement Function (SEF) has been added to the existing stability control augmentation system. The result is similar in effect to the fly-by-wire system used in the F-16, and by permitting safe controlled flight in what would otherwise be unstable regions of the flight envelope, will expand the envelope out to a full heavyweight condition. Manufactured by Sperry to a Rockwell design, SEF is first scheduled to fly in No 9, where it will be proved, and will be featured in production line aircraft from No 19 onward. SEF will also be retrofitted to the earlier aircraft at some unspecified date.

The defensive avionic system is scheduled for a thorough workout in the first quarter of 1986, using the B-1A and the first production B-1B. It is to be subjected to a carefully programmed sequence of tests against simulated threat environments with both the variety and intensity of the emissions gradually increasing. Operational integration with AWACS will also take place at some stage, while the tail warning radar will be tested against simulated airborne interceptions. Finally, the DAS will be evaluated against a hostile multi-threat environment.

Weapons trials will continue, and the first carriage and launch trials with ALCM are scheduled to commence in August 1986, lasting for 13 months. These will of course use B-1B No 9, which will be joined by No 28, which should become available from October 31, 1986, and which has been designated to carry out extra ALCM trials and also weapons development work with new, stealthy cruise missiles.

The loss of the second B-1A had little or no effect on the test programme, which is on target for IOC by July 1986. The crash, did, however, cause modifications to the FCGMS to be considered. In the manual mode, mishandling of which led to the disaster, an out-of-cg condition causes an orange light to illuminate as a warning: this light is located low on the dash, and it is believed that it may have been obscured by the crewmen's knees. Following modifications the light is now red, and from aircraft No 19 on it is being relocated to the glareshield, directly in the pilot's line of vision, while an aural warning has also been added in the form of a horn, and neither light nor horn can be switched off until the out-of-cg condition has been corrected.

Automatic-to-manual

Another modification involves the procedure for changing from automatic to manual modes. In the original system a free-floating toggle switch was used, but this has been replaced, again from No 19 onward, by a double-action lever lock switch. Both modifications will be retrofitted to the earlier B-1Bs in due course.

A further modification, proposed but still not implemented by early 1986, is the adoption of a wing sweep detent, a mechanical stop similar to that used in the F-111. Pumping fuel around the bomber is all very well, but it takes a certain amount of time, and in the manual mode sufficient time may not be allowed. The detent is a reminder to the pilot to check the cg position before sweeping the wings further; it works by stiffening the wing sweep control so that the pilot needs steadily increasing force to move it, until it will physically go no further while an out-of-cg condition exists. It will of course adjust as the fuel transfers and the cg position shifts. Rockwell have also suggested that a voice warning system could be adopted in lieu of the horn. This would be rather similar to the system used in the F-15, but if it is adopted it can hardly be built in on the production line before No 32, which will leave a lot of retrofitting to do.

Several incidents have occurred involving foreign object damage (FOD) to the engines, mainly to the fan blades. A few of these have been mysterious, with material similar to that used in the aircraft being found in the engines although nothing has been missing, and improved

Right: The second production B-1B touches down at Offutt AFB on June 27, 1985. Scheduled to fly on to Dyess two days later it suffered FOD during the landing and the No 1 B-1B took its place.

inspection procedures on the production line have been instituted as a preventative measure.

One incident involving B-1B No 1 was fairly straightforward. An avionics compartment forward of the intakes contains a special rack for test equipment, and a loose bolt from the rack came out from the compartment through a louvred cover. At least, so it appears: little FOD material was found in the engine, but what there was matched that of the missing bolt. A fix was easily found involving a new louvred cover with smaller slots.

At least two other FOD incidents have involved the air cooler flapper doors, which control the flow of air through ram air ducts for the environmental control system. At speeds exceeding Mach 0.45 the flapper doors, which at 5in by 7in (127mm by 178mm) are quite small, open to permit the entry of ram air; below this speed a sensor-controlled hydraulic powered blower fan forces the doors to close as the ram air flow diminishes. In both cases the doors appeared to have come apart in flight, and as they were located forward and between each pair of engines the debris had been ingested.

One incident came at a rather embarrassing moment. B-1B No 2 was the much heralded first operational aircraft to enter Strategic Air Command service, and was due to be handed over with great ceremony at Dyess AFB, Texas, on June 29, 1985, but as it came in to land at SAC Headquarters at Offutt AFB, Nebraska, on June 28 the flapper doors duly came unglued and FODed both engines on one side. Of course the aircraft was grounded as a result, and No 1 had to be flown post-haste from Edwards for the handover. The ceremony was duly performed; some 50,000 spectators had a great day out, and the only harm done was to the accuracy of some of the Press reports.

However minor the cause, engine FOD is a potentially dangerous problem, so measures were immediately put in hand to cure it and with typical American thoroughness, these were implemented in three phases. Phase I addressed the immediate problem of keeping the aircraft flying, and consisted of securing the existing assembly by using thicker bolts, extra washers, and locking wires. Phase II was instituted to find out whether the cheap and easy Phase I solution could be made permanent: the plan is to fix instruments to the left engine nacelle of the No 4 B-1A in order to find out exactly what aerodynamic forces are operating within the duct to cause the failures. Phase III is a Rockwell redesign of the flapper door assembly to reduce the number of parts, in case Phase II shows that Phase I can only be an interim solution.

One of the latest B-1B revisions concerns the life support systems. Oxygen for the crew is normally carried in cylinders in the form of liquid oxygen (lox), or as high pressure gas. An added hazard in a crash or battle situation, these are being replaced with a recently developed oxygen generating system by Normalair-Garrett, which draws sufficient oxygen from the engine bleed air by using a Zeolite nitrogen filtering system.

First operational base

Dyess AFB, near Abilene, Texas, was announced as the home of the first operational B-1B bomber unit by President Reagan on January 21, 1983. The resident 96th Bomb Wing consisted of two squadrons, the 337th Bomb Squadron, equipped with B-52H Stratofortresses, and the 917th Air Refuelling Squadron with KC-135A Stratotankers. The B-52s were phased out between August 1984 and January 1985 to make way for their replacement, while the tanker unit prepared to develop in-flight

Above: The bomb bay doors are highlighted during a test flight. Only the forward bay is long enough to accommodate the 20.8ft (6.3m) length of the ALCM.

Below: The rotary launcher used for SRAMs and B-61 nuclear bombs is capable of carrying eight weapons with a combined total weight of 25,000lb (11,340kg).

Left: The crew access ladder is located immediately behind the nosewheel: in an alert the crew would be expected to get aboard and have the aircraft off the ground in a matter of minutes.

defended targets, and critics have often asked why this could not be left to the ICBM and SLBM forces – why, in fact, a manned bomber was needed at all. To summarize what was written in the opening chapter, the ICBMs were felt to be too vulnerable to a preemptive strike, which if successful would leave no retaliatory capacity, while the SLBMs suffered from lack of accuracy, and in any case only a relatively small proportion of missile submarines would be on station at any one time, vastly reducing the striking power of the force as a whole. A further, less immediate consideration was the possibility that a sudden major improvement in submarine detection methods could render the entire SLBM force vulnerable to destruction before it could be used.

With those factors in mind, the manned bomber represented a second chance. A combination of dispersal and rapid reaction time should ensure that enough of the manned bomber force survives a surprise attack to represent a credible threat, and the force also represents a second-strike capability, unlike the other two delivery systems, which by their very nature are one-shot. As a delivery system, the manned bomber was accurate and flexible, capable of being retargeted or even recalled in mid-mission.

It should also be remembered that the manned bomber is the only proven method of nuclear weapon delivery, and in these days of heavy reliance on technology it is as well to remember that no-one really knows what would happen if the superpowers engaged in an all-out nuclear exchange. Certain conventional weapons have achieved remarkable results in the sterile, laboratory-like conditions of the test range, then failed to deliver the goods in combat.

Moreover, discussion of a limited nuclear exchange is arrant rubbish. When dealing with weapons of such destructive capability, a good analogy is that of a farmer giving a pig a condition pill: the pill is placed in a tube, which is inserted into the pig's mouth, and the farmer then blows down the tube, whereupon the pig swallows the pill. The trick is to make sure that the pig doesn't blow first! To apply the analogy to the current strategic situation, the pills are in place and the tubes firmly inserted, with both sides waiting for the first sign that the other is taking a deep breath.

It has been estimated that there are between 1,800 and 2,300 major targets in the Soviet Union, and that for the manned bomber to be a credible deterrent in its own right it should be capable of delivering some 2,000 nuclear weapons accurately on targets, regardless of where they are situated. In the majority of cases, this calls for deep penetration.

The cruise missile, for which the B-1 was nearly discarded, does not have the range to be effective, while its penetration capability against the Soviet defences has always been in question. There is a great difference between penetrating a hundred miles of hostile territory and a thousand. The Tercom terrain matching system is also susceptible to the vagaries of the Russian winter, as in many areas deep snow and iced-up rivers and estuaries would alter the appearance of the terrain, making matching difficult if not impossible. The difference between human and computer intelligence lies in the fact that the

Above: Maintenance personnel infiltrate the wing glove fairing to work on the central hydraulic reservoir, which is located above and between the engines.

refuelling techniques for the B-1B. The 337th will also be responsible for instructing other tanker units which are part of future B-1B equipped wings.

As the first B-1B unit, the 96th BMW will differ slightly in composition from the ordinary. The 337th ES will be the first standard operational squadron, but it will be preceded into service by the 4018th Combat Crew Training Squad-

ron, a dedicated aircrew training unit which was activated at Dyess on March 15, 1985. Also based at Dyess is Detachment 1 of the 4201st Test and Evaluation Squadron from Edwards. This unit is responsible for follow-on testing and evaluation on the B-1B and also for training the cadre of B-1B instructors assigned to the 4018th CCTS. The 4201st detachment will have no aircraft specifically assigned to them, but will use those of the 4018th, some 15 aircraft initially, notwithstanding that other seemingly authoritative sources put the figure at 10.

The 96th BW will take 11 aircraft on strength at first, plus three spares, a total

three less than the normal squadron establishment of 16, plus one spare, though it will have a full complement of 22 operational crews. Doubtless this situation will regularize itself when the training role of the 4018th CCTS diminishes, as it will when all units are up to strength and the requirement is reduced to the replacement of time-expired crews. Delivery of the 100th and last B-1B was originally scheduled for July or August 1988, but has now been brought forward to April 30 of that year.

The original mission envisaged for the B-1A was the deep penetration of the Soviet Union to make precision strikes on

Unrefuelled mission (SRAM and gravity weapons)

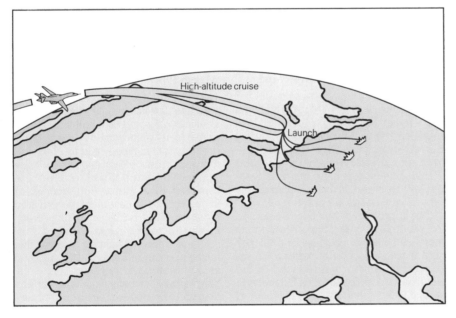

Above: One of the missions envisaged for the Long Range Combat Aircraft by the US Air Force bomber study group, set up to consider alternatives to the B-1A, involved the new high subsonic version of the B-1 carrying ALCMs in a high-altitude transatlantic return flight.

Right: Increased range, low observability and a more diverse payload were key features of the LRCA – subsequently the B-1B – so that the new bomber would be able to penetrate air defences at low level in support of theatre forces in Europe.

Unrefuelled mission (ALCMs)

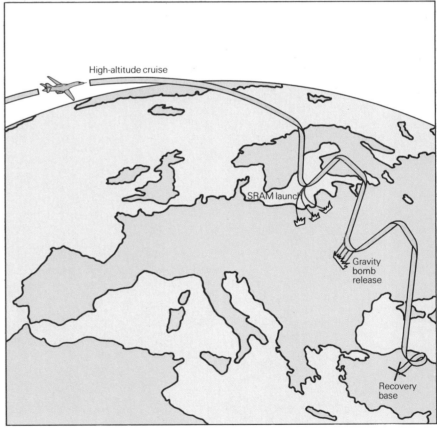

computer cannot have second thoughts, wonder whether it has just made a mistake and revise its judgement.

It has long been assumed that all strategic bomber bases in the United States are targeted by missiles, and in times of international tension the B-1 force is intended to be dispersed as widely as possible. There are at least 100 airfields capable of maintaining sustained B-1 operations, and another 250 FAA Grade III fields suitable for emergency dispersal – that is, sized for Boeing 727 type aircraft. The greatest threat comes from depressed trajectory SLBMs launched from just a few hundred

miles offshore, which would allow very little reaction time. The B-1, with its stand-alone capability, is intended to be able to take off and be several miles away from the airfield, hopefully beyond the worst effects of the nuclear detonation, within just four minutes of the warning being given.

The B-1A was intended to take off with a full weapons load, but just enough fuel to take it to cruising altitude and a rendezvous with a tanker. This gave a reasonable certainty of the survival of a fair number of the bombers, but placed a premium on the survival of the tanker force, without which the bombers were

impotent. It hardly needs saying that the tanker force could not be dispersed as widely or scrambled as quickly as the B-1s, and was therefore the weak link in the chain.

Crew/endurance limit

In the early days of the B-1 design period, when provision was to be made for two instructors as well as the four man crew, it was suggested that two extra crew could be carried, giving a maximum endurance of 36 hours with in-flight refuelling. This seems never to have been pursued, perhaps because the proposed number of B-1As, 244 in all,

was too low to allow flying what amounted to standing patrols in times of crisis.

The B-1A was to continue its mission by taking on a full load of fuel from the tanker, climbing to altitude and cruising at Mach 0.85 to the edge of the threat area. Depending on the tactical circumstances, it would then penetrate at Mach 2 at high altitude or descend to very low level for a high subsonic penetration. Where possible it would try to bypass the defences; if this was impracticable SRAMs would be launched to suppress them. Nuclear gravity weapons would normally be carried as part of a weapons mix for use against major targets, as

Left: With wings fully swept for low-level penetration, the B-1B is literally faster than a speeding bullet. Full operation at the 200ft (60m) penetration altitude had not been demonstrated by the time the first operational aircraft was delivered.

Above: Wings fully forward is the normal position for landing, but the second B-1B landed successfully with the wings at 55° when a fault caused the wings to stick in that position during a training flight from Dyess in March 1986.

these generally had a greater yield than the smaller warheads carried by the missiles. The fuel consumed in Mach 2 penetration naturally reduced the operational radius substantially, and would have been used for relatively shallow penetration missions over the less heavily defended areas.

The approach to the mission adopted for the B-1B was far more realistic: its increased fuel tankage gave a 25 per cent increase in operational radius; its reliance on tankers was reduced by the fact that it can take off with a full fuel and weapons load, and has an unrefuelled range described as intercontinental; stealth and eluding the defences became much more important; and the Mach 2 requirement was dropped. The B-1B still retains a supersonic capability – Mach 1.4 to be precise – but this is largely residual, nice to have but rarely likely to be of any great value.

From a practical point of view, it is always easier to see the apparent short-comings of one's own equipment than to assess objectively the problems it poses to the other side, and it is wise to slightly overrate the capabilities of an opponent until exact assessment is possible. While SAC has been concerned with such matters as reasonable attrition rates and mission success probabilities, the Soviet defence forces must have been very concerned about their chances of preventing both the B-1A and the B-1B from inflicting unacceptable damage.

Frankly, to talk about attrition rates in an all-out nuclear war can only be an academic exercise, but one useful consequence of the B-1 programme is that while the B-1B is an extremely costly machine, the cost of an even half-way

effective defence against it for a country as vast in area and as lengthy in border as the Soviet Union would be many times greater, both in money and in effort, and the resources expended in defence against this one threat cannot be directed elsewhere. But success or failure for the B-1B will be determined by whether it ever has to fly its primary mission: if it does, it has failed.

It is a truism of military aviation that hardware optimized for one function usually ends up doing something else. Many aircraft of many nations have been designed as nuclear weapon delivery systems, but, fortunately, not one has ever been used for that purpose. Some have been engaged in reconnaissance; others have ended their lives as tankers; and just a few – the B-52 and the Vulcan spring to mind – have dropped some conventional iron bombs.

The B-1B seems to be heading the same way. It is now proposed to use it for a variety of missions, including maritime reconnaissance and mine laying, anti-shipping attacks using smart weapons such as Harpoon, and conventional interdiction. Official statements credit it with the ability to extend US Navy capability in both coastal and inland power projection, and with its range and payload it could bring force to bear until orthodox tactical reinforcements arrived.

It also seems probable that the B-1B may be used as part of the US Army Air/Land Battle doctrine, which requires rapid reaction to a superior enemy force on the battlefield, and would involve both hitting the attack spearhead and massive attacks against the support echelons which kept it supplied. It is also reported that plans are afoot for the B-1B force to interdict Warsaw Pact airfields to take the pressure off NATO fighter and strike aircraft and free them for the close air support mission. This mission could be flown from bases in the United States, presumably at fairly high altitude using stand-off weapons.

The last mission, however, would indeed be a desperate measure. Bearing in mind the colossal cost of a single B-1B and the severely limited numbers being acquired, it is very hard to envisage a situation outside total war where the loss of even one could be justified. It is also difficult to conceive of a conventional war situation even in central Europe where the B-1B could do a better job than equal-cost quantities of Tornados, or even F-111s, although the answer to this may emerge by the end of the decade: the SAC bombing competition is an annual event, and after Tornado teams from the RAF swept the board in the 1984 and 1985 competitions it is reasonable to assume that the B-1B will be entered as soon as the USAF thinks it has a fair chance of reclaiming some of its silverware.

Achieving Initial Operational Capability (IOC) in July 1986, the B-1B is scheduled to carry the burden of penetration for some ten years, at which point the Advanced Technology Bomber (ATB) is due to enter service. This new machine, using the very latest stealth techniques, will then take over the penetrator role, and the B-1B will revert to being a stand-off cruise missile carrier replacing the elderly B-52s. It should last in this mission from 1995 to approximately 2010. But will it?

The ATB, under development by Northrop, is variously rumoured to look like a cross between a wide-span Vulcan and the old Northrop flying wings; it is also rumoured to be small, with less carrying capacity than the B-1B. Certainly it will be more expensive; equally certainly it will have more than its fair share of detractors. Almost certainly history will repeat itself, and the ATB will be rubbished in favour of the more effective, low technical risk, and much cheaper B-1B – or, as it may well be, the B-1C or B-1D.

Handling properties

B-1B handling is reported to be very good, although little detail has been given, probably because unlike a fighter which has been designed to be hurled around the sky, the sedate manoeuvring required of the LRCA is not exciting by comparison. The cockpit features a stick rather than the wheel common to most large aircraft, and each pilot has a left-hand throttle quadrant. Major George W. Larson Jr gave an account of his impressions to *Air Force Magazine* in June 1976:

"Taxiing the aircraft is easy with nosewheel steering through the rudder pedals. Smooth, positive differential braking is effective in the event of a nosewheel steering malfunction. The old groaning and screeching and shuddering associated with other large aircraft braking systems is not evident. With the wings at full forward sweep, 15°, slats extended, and full flaps, the B-1 is configured for takeoff . . . in full augmentor there is a smooth, rapid acceleration to liftoff speed. Only minimum aft stick

displacement is needed at rotation speed, and you find yourself airborne in approximately 3,000 to 4,000ft (914 to 1,219m). After takeoff retrimming is necessary as the flaps are retracted. . . Manoeuvring the aircraft in pitch or roll is a pleasant surprise. Only small control displacements (one or two inches depending on airspeed) are required. The response to a control stick input is rapid. There are no sluggish or delayed control responses. . . Refuelling the B-1 is much easier [than earlier large bombers]. Only very minimal control inputs are required, thrust response is rapid and effective, and visibility is excellent.

"[In low level flight] the already rapid control responses increase in this high dynamic pressure regime. . . In the traffic pattern, the B-1 is so responsive

you can fly an ILS or an overhead pattern with equal ease and precision. Some pilot adaptation is required prior to touchdown on landing. I consistently feel that I'm higher than necessary when the main gear touches down. The reason is that the pilot sits considerably forward of the main landing gear and is flying the aircraft at an angle of attack of approximately seven degrees during the landing flare. While it makes a grease job more demanding, it does not detract from easily landing the aircraft."

Nor is the B-1B's handling in any way inferior. Air Force Chief Test Pilot Lt Col Leroy Schroeder has commented that handling is so good that "sometimes you've got to stop and think how big this aircraft is before you do some things because it handles so well."

Strategic bomber force modernization

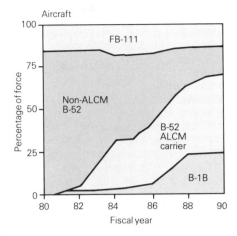
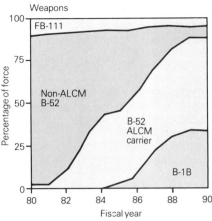

Left: Badge and motto of the 96th Bomb Wing, whose 4018th Combat Crew Training Squadron and 337th Bomb Squadron are the first operational users of the B-1B. The 96th is at Dyess AFB, near Abilene, Texas.

Below: Silhouetted against the rays of the setting sun, a B-1B refuels from a KC-135. Fuel and aircrew costs have made the idea of maintaining standing patrols with the B-1B a non-starter.

Above: By 1990 B-1Bs and ALCM-equipped B-52s will represent, respectively, 25 and 45 per cent of SAC's bomber force, and the combination will be responsible for over 85 per cent of its weapons.

Glossary and abbreviations

ACES Advanced Concept Ejection Seat
acronym name composed of initial letters
AFB Air Force Base (USAF, continental USA only)
AFCS Automatic Flight Control System
AFSC Air Force Systems Command
AGE Automatic Ground Environment (defensive system)
ALCM Air Launched Cruise Missile
algorithm mathematical formula or process
AMP Advanced Manned Penetrator
AMPSS Advanced Manned Penetrating Strategic System
AMSA Advanced Manned Strategic Aircraft
AMT Accelerated Mission Testing
anhedral downward angle of horizontal flying surfaces
APU Auxiliary Power Unit
ARS Air Refuelling Squadron
aspect ratio ratio of span² to wing area
ATB Advanced Technology Bomber
beam sharpening radar technique giving better definition over a small area
BMAC Boeing Military Airplane Company
body lift lift gained from the fuselage area rather than from the wings
BPE Bomber Penetration Evaluation
breadboard experimental layout for electronic system
bypass ratio ratio of total air passing through the engine against that passing through the core section
BW Bomb Wing
CCTS Combat Crew Training Squadron
CED Continued Engineering Development
CITEPS Central Integrated Test Expert Parameter System

CITS Central Integrated Test System
CMCA Cruise Missile Carrier Aircraft
CRT Cathode Ray Tube
CSRL Common Strategic Rotary Launcher
dihedral upward angle of horizontal flying surfaces
DSARC Defense System Acquisition Review Council
DSO Defensive (avionics) System Officer
DVT Design Verification Testing
EAR Electronically Agile Radar
ECM Electronic Countermeasures
EMP Electromagnetic Pulse (from nuclear explosion)
empennage tail section
EMUX electronic multiplex
ERSA Extended Range Strategic Aircraft
Faraday Cage device for excluding unwanted electrical emissions
FBW Fly By Wire
FCGMS Fuel and Centre of Gravity Management System
FLIR Forward Looking Infra Red
FOD Foreign Object Damage (to engines)
fuel fraction proportion of fuel load to gross weight
GCI Ground Controlled Interception
gust response the reaction of the aircraft to rapid changes in wind direction and velocity
HF High Frequency
HP High Pressure
ICBM Intercontinental Ballistic Missile
IDR Initial Design Review
IFR In Flight Refuelling
ILS Instrument Landing System
incidence angle of attack
INS Inertial Navigation System
IOC Initial Operational Capability

IOTE Initial Operational Test and Evaluation
IR Infra-red
IRCM Infra-red Countermeasures
Lantirn Low altitude navigation and targetting infra-red at night
LAMP Low Altitude Manned Penetrator
LARC Low Altitude Ride Control
LLTV Low Light Television
LP Low Pressure
LRCA Long Range Combat Aircraft
LRU Line Replaceable Unit
MAC Mean Aerodynamic Chord
Mach Number Speed expressed in terms of the local speed of sound
MFD Multi-Function Display
MilSpec Military Specification
mockup full scale engineering model
MRB Multi-Role Bomber
NASA National Aeronautics and Space Agency
NATO North Atlantic Treaty Organization
NTP Near Term Penetrator
overpressure the difference between the aircraft internal pressure and the air pressure externally in the vicinity of a nuclear blast
PFRT Preliminary Flight Rating Test
PIRA Precision Impact Range Area
pitch movement about the vertical longitudinal axis
psi pounds per square inch
prf pulse repetition frequency (radar)
PVP Production Verification Program
q dynamic pressure
QT Qualification Test
R & D Research and Development
RAM Radar Absorbing Material
ramp hardstanding or apron
RCS Radar Cross-Section
red line 'never exceed' limits

SAC Strategic Air Command, USAF
SAM Surface to Air Missile
SAR Synthetic Aperture Radar
SCAD Subsonic Cruise Armed Decoy
SDT System Development Tool
SEAT Status Evaluation and Test
SEF Stability Enhancement Function
SIS Stall Inhibitor System
SLAB Subsonic Low Altitude Bomber
SLBM Submarine Launched Ballistic Missile
SMCS Structural Mode Control System
spoilers roll control surfaces which 'dump" lift
SRAM Short Range Attack Missile
stabilizers tail flying surfaces
static thrust the thrust produced by the engines when stationary at ground level
SWL Strategic Weapons Launcher
Tacan Tactical air navigation
telemetry the relaying of information from instruments to ground receivers during a test flight
TES Test and Evaluation Squadron
Tercom Terrain contour matching
TOGW Take Off Gross Weight
TREES Transient Response of Electronic Equipment and systems (to a nuclear detonation)
Triad The three nuclear deterrent delivery systems
V-G variable geometry (actually variable sweep)
VHF Very High Frequency
VTOL Vertical Take Off and Landing
WCT box Wing Carry Through box

Deployment

PAA: Primary Aircraft Authorized
BAI: Back-up Aircraft Inventoried
FI: Flight Instructional
OP: Operational
IOC: Initial Operational Capability

Base	Activated	First delivery	Equipment complete	IOC	Unit	PAA	BAI	Crews
Dyess AFB, Texas	Mar 85	29 Jun 85	Nov 86	Sep 86	4018 CCTS	15	—	18 FI
					96 BW	11	3	22 OP
Ellsworth AFB, South Dakota	Oct 86	Dec 86	Jul 87	N/A	28 BW	32	3	44 OP
Grand Forks AFB, North Dakota	Feb 87	Aug 87	Jan 88	N/A	319 BW	16	1	22 OP
McConnell AFB, Kansas	Jul 87	Jan 88	30 Apr 88	N/A	384 BW	16	1	22 OP

Authorized strength: 90 aircraft plus 8 back-ups plus 2 at Edwards AFB (4200th TES) = 100 Total.

Specifications

Dimensions (ft/m)	B-1A	B-1B
Length (B-1A inc probe)	151.17/46.07	147/44.80
Height	33.58/10.23	34/10.36
Span at 15° sweep	136.67/41.65	137/41.76
Span at 67½° sweep	78.17/23.83	78/23.77
Main gear track	14.50/4.42	14.50/4.42
Wing area ft²/m²	1,950/181.2	1,950/181.2

Weights (lb/kg)		
Empty, approx	172,000/78,019	172,000/78,019
Gross takeoff	395,000/179,172	477,000/216,367
Max weapons load	115,000/52,164	125,000/56,700

Performance		
Speed lo	Mach 0.85	Mach 0.85
Speed hi	Mach 2.22	Mach 1.40
Ceiling (ft/m)	50,000/15,240 plus	49,000/14,934
Range unrefuelled (nm/km)	5,200/9,636	6,500/12,045

Power	Engines	4xF101-GE-100
4xF101-GE-102	Dry rating (lb/kN)	17,000/75.6
17,000/75.6	Wet rating (lb/kN)	30,000/133
30,000/133		

Production

Lot	Aircraft	Serials		Tail codes	
I	1	82–0001		20001	
II	2–8	83–0065	0071	30065	30071
III	9–19	84–0049	0059	40049	40059
IV	20–54	85–0062	0096	50062	50096
V	55–100	N/A		N/A	

Picture credits

Don't miss these exciting titles in the ARCO MODERN FIGHTING AIRCRAFT SERIES at your local bookstore or order today using the coupon below

☐ YES, please send me the following MODERN FIGHTING AIRCRAFT TITLES:

TIC	VOL#	TITLE	PRICE	QUANTITY
65-05902	1	F-15 EAGLE	12.95	_____
65-05903	2	F-16 FIGHTING FALCON	12.95	_____
65-05904	3	F-111	11.95	_____
65-06068	4	F-4 PHANTOM	12.95	_____
65-06069	5	THE HARRIER	11.95	_____
65-06070	6	A-10 THUNDERBOLT	11.95	_____
65-06071	7	F/A-18 HORNET	12.95	_____
65-06406	8	F-14 TOMCAT	12.95	_____
65-06493	9	MIGS	12.95	_____
67-92550	10	TORNADO	12.95	_____
67-05523	11	B-1B	12.95	_____
67-02076	12	AH-64	12.95	_____
67-02075	13	AH-1	12.95	_____

Prices subject to change
without notice.

Merchandise Total	$	_____
Add Sales Tax (for your state)	$	_____
Add 12% Postage & Handling*	$	_____
Total: Check Enclosed	$	_____

SEND YOUR ORDER TO:

SIMON & SCHUSTER
MAIL ORDER BILLING
Route 59 at Brook Hill Drive
West Nyack, New York 10994

☐ PLEASE CHARGE MY ☐ MASTERCARD ☐ VISA
Credit Card # _____
Expiration
date _____ Signature _____

☐ ENCLOSED IS MY CHECK OR MONEY ORDER
  *Publisher pays postage & handling charges for prepaid
   and charge card orders.

☐ BILL ME

NAME _____
ADDRESS _____ APT. # _____
CITY _____ STATE _____ ZIP _____

IMPORTANT: Enclose check with order, price plus applicable sales tax for your state (unless being billed).
Please allow four weeks for delivery.